WAR AND PEST

FROM BASRA TO BEDBUGS

Michael Coates

FOREWORD

Good leaders build stronger teams. And stronger teams grow successful businesses.

But what systems do you need to put in place for this to happen? How do you help your team to grow and flourish? How can you become a better leader and positively impact the world around you?

This book will show you how.

It's full of the life lessons that Michael and I have learned over 17 years working together in the Royal Engineers and later in our respective careers (mine in the Special Forces, combatting piracy in the Indian Ocean and Michael in the fire service, protecting the public from life threatening danger.)

We show you how to take the skills from the battlefield into business. Whether you lead a team, own a business or manage an organisation, you can use the SEARCH methodology to become a better leader, create an interdependent culture and positively impact the world around you.

Lift everyone together and everyone achieves more.

Des Fraser

Des Fraser
Co-founder of Combat Pest Control & Declassified
Former Special Forces Soldier
Operations Specialist

CONTENTS

Introduction   8

Section 1 – Who we are   12

The Combat DNA   13

Our Ethos   14

Our Values   18

Our Vision   22

Declassified   32

Section 2 – Learning to lead with
the SEARCH method   40

Interdependent Leadership   41

Leadership Systems   44

Leadership Education   46

Leadership Accountability   48

Leadership Risk   52

Leadership Control   56

Leadership Help   60

Section 3 – Combatting pests
with the SEARCH method   62

Introduction   63

System   64

Education   70

Rats   71

Mice   75

Clothes Moths   78

Bedbugs   80

Fleas   82

Oriental Cockroaches   84

German Cockroaches   86

Wasps   88

Black Garden Ants   90

Pharaoh Ants   92

Cluster Flies   94

Blow Flies   95

Fruit Flies   96

Sewage Flies   97

Grey Squirrels   98

Foxes   100

Feral Pigeons   102

Other Household Pests   104

Food Handling and Pest Control   108

Accountability 112

Risk 116

Control 124

Rats 127

Mice 127

Clothes Moths 128

Bedbugs 128

Fleas 129

Oriental Cockroaches 130

German Cockroaches 130

Squirrel 131

Wasps 131

Ants 132

Cluster Flies 132

Blow Flies 133

Fruit Flies 133

Drain Flies 134

Foxes 134

Feral Pigeon 135

Help 136

Acknowledgements 152

The Author 154

For the last 4 years, I have been fascinated by how companies work and how service is provided.

What has intrigued me most is that very few organisations look at themselves as anything more than a service provider. They are concerned with their own profits and gains, and rarely look beyond this to see a bigger picture. Taking, but never giving back.

Why interdependency matters

My experience as a soldier has taught me that the key to success in any mission is interdependency: the ability to work together to reach an end objective.

By aligning values with other like-minded people and by having a genuine interest in the success of a partnered organisation and those within it, the outcomes are significantly improved for all concerned. Put simply, we can achieve more together than any of us could on our own.

Experience has taught us that applying a methodology which creates interdependency, either in a team, an organisation, or across a sector (such as social housing), can have a transformative effect on solving difficult issues, finding new solutions or achieving a shared goal.

Establishing interdependency

On the 7th January 2000, aged 16, I boarded a train leaving Hull station and embarked on a huge adventure. I arrived at the Army apprentice college, ready for a career in the British Army.

My first few days and weeks were all about the basics. Understanding systems and working to procedures, absorbing information, learning about accountability (either as an individual or a group), assessing risk within a military environment, using control measures to get results and understanding why working interdependently and asking for help is vital to the successful completion of a shared objective.

Weeks turned into months, months turned into years and in 2003, aged 19, I arrived in Kuwait, fully trained and ready. At the time I didn't know it, but over the course of the next year, the experiences I would have, the relationships I would forge, and the lessons I would learn, would stay with me forever.

Operation Telic was the code name used for military operations during the second Gulf war and I, along with many thousand of young soldiers, crossed the border from Kuwait to Iraq.

During conflict, when things get hostile and uncomfortable, there are six key principles to stick to. These create interdependency and can be adapted to any group of organisations seeking to achieve a shared aim. The most important part of creating a fully functioning team is leadership. The way we conduct ourselves, treat others and organise our business or organisation has a huge impact on how we all collectively pull together.

At Combat, we call this our SEARCH methodology. You can read about it in Sections 2 and 3.

Why interdependency is key in social housing (my sector example)

I have spent most of my childhood in social housing.

But the world is changing. Our cities are growing. Our population is rising. Our councils' resources are ever more stretched. Each of these factors are contributing to the rise in pest problems.

I wanted to write this book to help empower social housing residents, housing trusts, associations and their partner companies to ensure we collectively secure properties that are not only fit for human habitation but allow communities to thrive.

Urbanisation and the rise in population has done many great things for the country. Our communities have never been so diverse. Our collective culture has been enriched as a result. We can eat what we like, travel where we please. We live in a time where there is a service for everything.

However, according to Newton's third law: for every action, there is an equal and opposite reaction.

For all the advantages these things bring, there are very real risks.

Take household waste collections. Dwindling council resources mean that times between the refuse pick-ups are stretched from weekly to fortnightly. More waste sits on our streets for longer and gives rise to more pests.

In the advent of the housing crisis, many thousands of homes have been quickly built, often in close proximity to each other, which allows pests to spread more rapidly.

World travel has expanded our minds. But it's also introduced a global dispersal of pests, from one continent to another. It's a problem that doesn't discriminate.

The rise in population, urbanisation, world travel and tighter local authority budgets has led to a significant rise in pests. From rats in our streets, to mice in our homes and bedbugs feasting on us in shared housing. We are very much at war.

We do have options to combat pests in our homes. Many councils offer a low budget pest control service. Private companies offer a myriad of treatments that often get clear results. Or you can manage it yourself.

Pest infestations can cause great stress and anxiety. Our home is our castle but when it's invaded we can feel hostages or prisoners in the place where we live.

I grew up in a low income family with a very house-proud mother, which meant, quite often, a DIY approach to many tasks had to be carried out.

So I wrote a full section in this book to give everyone the chance to make informed decisions, understand the systems and procedures involved to help prevent infestations happening in your home or a property you are responsible for.

Section 3 of WAR AND PEST will enable you to combat pests in your home. It offers guidance, advice and best practice but will also highlight unsafe areas where physical professional work should be carried out.

This book will also talk you through my journey in business and our SEARCH methodology. Together, these sections create an interdependent system that allows you to achieve more.

WHO WE ARE

WAR AND PEST

THE COMBAT DNA

In 2015, we starting hearing whispers. Whispers that some of our close friends, friends of friends, peers and seniors were suffering. Suffering from injury and illness sustained in conflict. Since 2000*, operations in Iraq, Afghanistan, Sierra Leone and many other areas have really taken its toll on our military community and some of the after-effects were now surfacing.

In December 2015, Des (my friend and business partner) and I sat down and discussed what we could do to help. We decided to set up a company. The initial idea was to give away profit to military charities. But what if we didn't make a profit? And did business actually work like that? Were you left with a pot of cash at the end of the week, month or year?

We were determined to make a difference. So we sat at my kitchen table and asked ourselves: what organisation would we want to work with? What do we stand for? And why would we do what we do?

We started by writing down our vision. We'll tell you more about this shortly. But put simply, this organisation was founded with the simple belief that we had to help others.

Next, we defined our values.

Now, I've known Des since 2001 and we've been through a lot together - from Iraq to the rugby field and now business. I knew that our values aligned. But what about our company's values?

Values are what sets us apart and what brings us, and those around us, closer together. Having a set of values that we agree to hold ourselves to and make business decisions around makes life significantly easier.

The next thing was to create an ethos. This ethos was to become the bedrock of who we were and how the company would run. At this time I was a serving firefighter and Des was working to combat piracy in the Indian Ocean. We looked at all the industries we had worked in. We cherry picked the good and dug deep into the bad. We didn't want our foundations to be off-set. We wanted them to be simple, clear and strong.

* I have only referred to operations since 2000 as this is the generation that I served in and have direct experience of. This is not to say that operations before or after have also generated their own injuries or illnesses. Nor am I discrediting the service of those who served before or after this period.

OUR ETHOS

WAR AND PEST

Our Ethos

There is a certain order to our ethos, it has to remain in the order set out and cannot (even for one minute) be mixed up. This is our foundation.

Step 1

Look after yourself and your family – this is absolutely vital in creating a happy and productive environment. Coming from a military background, many of our current team members have spent vast amounts of time away from their loved ones. So we are absolutely driven to ensure everyone in the company gets the right amount of work/life balance. As I write this, everyone in the company works a 4 day week, basic standards like the London living wage are in place and we have a weekly fruit and vegetable allowance. Each year, we encourage everyone to participate in an active fundraising event (and we pay the entry fee). If any of our team need time off for a family event, then we work to accommodate that request.

Sometimes it's the simple things that go along way. For example, take our latest member of the team. She is very competent, capable and driven. She's married to a current serving British Army Officer who recently deployed on operations to Cyprus. We have found ways for her to fulfill her role flexibly, so that when the opportunity arises for her to spend time with him, she can – by working remotely in Cyprus or managing her 4 day week flexibly. This will make her military life significantly easier – now and in the future

Step 2

Protect the company and our clients - once we've taken care of ourselves, then we can start protecting others. We take pride in how we work together and how we look after our clients. Having a frontline team made up exclusively of military veterans creates cohesion and an overriding ability to succeed together.

Our team are remarkable and I thank them all for what they do every day. Their drive and commitment has enabled us to provide industry-leading solutions to our clients' problems. A great example of this is when we helped an elderly gentleman with a severe bedbug infestation. When I say severe, I mean the worst bedbug infestation I have seen in my career. We were 100% committed to giving him back his clean, pest-free home – not to mention his quality of life and his dignity. Even though we faced many dilemmas in this case, it took time, thoroughness, co-operation, understanding of the situation and the ability to adapt throughout the task to achieve success.

Step 3

Care for the wider military and local community - extremely important part of our identity is understanding and implementing care for our fellow military veterans and for those in our local community who need it most. We take this seriously and over the past few years we have seen examples ranging from fund raising events for military charities, responding to severe pest control incidents (for free) involving vulnerable adults at risk and engaging with the Ministry of Defence to actively help and advocate veteran employment. We are the smallest and youngest organisation to have ever won the Ministry of Defence gold award in employer recognition scheme. We often join forces with other forces friendly companies who wish to provide opportunity and support to our military community. Oh, and we also present a podcast but more about that later.

Step 4

Take responsibility for the greater good - when the first 3 steps of our ethos are achieved we can then look at the bigger picture. As a small company, we can still contribute to all sorts of global problems. Take the UN global goals for sustainable development. This sounds grand and out of reach for any micro or small business. But it's not. In fact, Small and Medium Sized Enterprises (SMEs) are more likely to have a bigger global impact, as long as we can work together as a collective.

The UN's global goals cover the 17 biggest threats our planet face. Small tasks carried out many times can produce amazing impact. Often, we see larger organisations in the press and media but if we delve into the subject of taking responsibility for the greater good then we see many, many smaller organisations taking ownership.

A great example of this is Buy1 Give1, an organisation based in Singapore whose sole purpose is to create a world full of giving. They enable small organisations to create life changing and enhancing impacts all around the world. Please look them up at B1G1.com

This organisation has opened our eyes to just what can be achieved by the many.

EMPLOY

MILITARY VETERANS & RESERVISTS

EDUCATE

AND ASSIST CHILDREN IN CONFLICT

PROTECT

OUR CLIENTS

SUPPORT

INJURED SERVICE PERSONNEL

OUR VALUES

WAR AND PEST

These are the 7 values that define us as a team and as individuals. Understanding what and who we are, then building a team around those points, has been crucial to the way we operate. It gives us a framework, a modus operandi, that we can use to make decisions – one that isn't monetised and prioritises values over value.

Without these, we would be nothing.

C

Commitment to the unrelenting pursuit of excellence

As simple as this sounds, it takes the most work. That's because, as a team, we are not content to sit still. We are driven to find new, better, more efficient ways of doing things. It's what bonds us together. And it's what our clients and partners have come to value about us. But in order for innovation to exist, you need to create the right conditions. Our team are not afraid to test, make mistakes, innovate and develop. Because we know that's the only way we'll continue to develop and grow.

O

Open minded

We never get sidetracked by what our competitors are up to. Some may say this is foolish. But from our point of view, why would we limit ourselves to what people in our own industry are doing when there's so much to learn from across the board? Whether that is how a brewery in Scotland gives away their recipes, to how a global retailer ensures outstanding customer service; or how the CEO of a large food handling organisation drives their team or how a ventilation company fit out branded restaurants. Even as a small company, we are constantly trying to evolve and the key to this is to stay open minded.

M

Mindful & respectful of others

We understand that everyone is different. How one individual may work or learn may be different to another. We believe that success is built on adapting to different needs and valuing what each person brings to the team. We respect everyone, regardless of their background or 'status'. Our policy is: first be mindful, offer respect, trust will follow.

B

Be happy

As basic as this seems, happiness is so important. Now I'm not talking about jumping around like a child fuelled on ice cream, but inner happiness is key to ensuring good physical and mental health. Being a supportive team member and employer plays a huge part. Creating an environment that promotes happiness and meaning will enable people to thrive.

Accountability

What we mean by this is creating clear roles and responsibilities, so everyone knows what they're accountable for. By doing this, we share a collective responsibility for a task, but have a clear role of the part we play in achieving it. When individuals within a team understand exactly what is needed then we remove the risk of confusion, which in turn creates more accountable communities.

To honour humility

Regardless of what we do in life, to honour humility and never forget why we are here, is something we stand by. Although we strive for excellence, we also remain humble. We know that we have a lot of work to do still and we will require lots of help and support along the way.

Self discipline

Implementing self-control and self discipline is almost a lifestyle and can make such a huge difference to you and those around you. It's about operating outside your 'comfort zone'. Pushing your own boundaries. This requires self-discipline. Small uncomfortable tasks, carried out frequently will provide something enjoyable at the end.

THIS IS
OUR VISION

WAR AND PEST

THIS IS OUR VISION

We employ veterans, reservists, military spouses and partners.

The first part of our vision is simple – employ our military veterans and reservists. This is our foundation and what sets us apart.

To create a good team is fairly easy, to create an outstanding team is a challenge. What members of the Armed Forces bring to our team (and to any team) is the ability to work interdependently.

The very essence of teamwork is to achieve a common goal, to ensure everyone is moving in the same direction.

Some people suggest that members of the Armed Forces are dependent upon someone else within their section, troop or squadron. This is not the case.

As humans we have 3 key stages of human development:

- **Dependancy** – to rely on another person and not be able to support yourself.

- **Independency** – not reliant on another and can self-support.

- **Interdependent** – to know and understand that everyone relies upon each other.

I could break it down like this:

A military team are on a patrol and have a particular task to carry out.

This team needs to work symbiotically of each other, otherwise the patrol will become inefficient and potentially fail. Too many independent people and the same could happen. When interdependency is evident and understood, the patrol achieve greater things. This means that everyone needs to understand that all members are as important as each other, and to achieve something special, all individuals must contribute to create that team.

This is why employing military veterans and reservists is so important to us. They understand why being interdependent is key to creating an amazing team.

We also believe in helping other organisations to work together interdependently, as we know much more can be achieved for the greater good – especially in the social housing sector. We champion this style of working and actively seek out partner organisations who share our values and passion for change.

EDUCATE & ASSIST

WAR AND PEST

Educate & Assist

This organisation was founded with the simple belief that we had to help others. The initial eight members of Combat had all experienced conflict and understood that, quite often, the most vulnerable people in war are children. My own experiences in Iraq in 2003 and the shared experiences of many of my friends have drawn us to two key areas.

The first is the education of street children in Afghanistan. Having discussed the issue with a long term friend Paul (a current serving member of the Royal Engineers), he explained how the situation in Afghanistan is particular bad. Especially for young boys who are most prone to sexual and physical abuse (research 'Bacha Bazi' for some fine journalistic examples which highlight this issue). Paul also explained the countless British lives saved by the Afghan youngsters who would regularly tip off troops and interpreters on the ground about locally known Taliban locations.

So our minds were made up. In March 2017, we started to impact the life of a street child every time we completed a job. One visit = one day of education through our global partners Buy 1 Give 1 (B1G1).

Secondly, we wanted to impact the lives of children affected by conflict globally. The statistics concerning landmine deaths and injuries worldwide are astonishing.

Over 60 states and countries still have hidden landmines, and it's estimated there are 110 million landmines in the ground. A landmine is the perfect soldier: ever courageous, never sleeps, never misses.

Nearly 9000 global accidents happen per year and almost 50% of those involve children who often play in unmarked minefields close to their homes. The threat is real and undiscriminating.

We wanted to use the power of our business to make a change.

So in October 2017, we partnered with APOPO. An organisation who train Giant African pouched rats to detect explosives within the ground. These rodents are not only accurate but also fast.

Our pledge is for each commercial task we carry out, we make a donation to APOPO which allows minefields to be cleared, creating a safe environment to live and play.

PROTECT OUR CUSTOMERS

WAR AND PEST

Protect our customers

There are some great pest management companies out there, many of whom I have worked with and would recommend to others. What sets us apart is our team and our world vision.

All our members are driven:

- To provide employment to veterans and reservists, spouses and partners.

- To provide education and assistance to children in conflict.

- To support injured service personnel.

- And of course, protect our clients regardless of how minor or severe the task.

Every single day, we test and develop new ways of operating to provide the best service to our customers and to achieve our wider vision.

We are committed to operational excellence. Doing the best job we can – every time. But we also believe in sharing our knowledge. We dedicate a large amount of our time to helping people understand how to get rid of pests themselves and how to prevent pest infestations in the future. We call it a pre-emptive strike – using proactive control measures to prevent any pest activity and maintain a safe and productive environment 365 days a year. This is one of the reasons why we wrote this book. It explains our methods and tactics around prevention, eradication and next steps. It's also why we've created a series of 'How to' videos on YouTube, too. To watch them for yourself, just search 'Combat Pest Control' on YouTube. Or visit us online at warandpest.com

Why do we share our knowledge?

The answer is simple. Our aim is to give everyone the opportunity to live without fear of pests in and around their home and their business – no matter where they live or what their income level is. We also want decision makers to understand what needs to be done.

SUPPORT OUR INJURED SERVICE PERSONNEL

WAR AND PEST

Support our injured service personnel

In recent years, our Armed Forces have engaged in several brutal conflicts. Conflicts that have left many injured. Some of those injuries are all too visible, including amputations and burns. But some scars are harder to see. Many are struggling with the debilitating effects of post-traumatic stress disorder, affecting their home life, working life and longterm mental health.

After serving their country, we believe that all those leaving the military should be given a fair opportunity in the workplace. And, for those with injuries, that opportunity should be without prejudice and they should face no disadvantage.

Our Declassified podcast has helped us (and many others) open the box on stigmatized conversations like PTSD, physical disability and more.

Since recording the podcasts, I believe now (more than ever) that those impacted by trauma and conflict can actually give more to the world of work. Why? It is due to a condition called post-traumatic growth – the phenomenon seen in those who have experienced trauma. Those who have survived a traumatic event become wiser, well-rounded and more accepting of others. This in turn creates a stronger person both inside and outside too

When it comes to supporting military veterans, there are some amazing people out there, doing amazing things. But as a national community, we need to become more interdependent. By working together, we can create the fairness and opportunity our Armed Forces veterans deserve.

The roll of big business has never been greater. Organisations who are forces friendly have a unique opportunity to guide, mentor and partner with smaller companies who share similar values and standards.

The government needs to keep engaging with industry. The Defence Relationship Management team (DRM) are doing a brilliant job. They work tirelessly to achieve their goal of creating long-term links between Armed Forces leavers and employers. But more needs to be done by small business owners who are dedicated to spreading the forces friendly word.

And finally, there are several charities working to provide employment opportunities including, The Poppy Factory, Walking With The Wounded and Mission Motor Sport to name a few. They share best practice to improve everything for everyone. Change is coming with many business, organisations, trusts and local authorities realising that our military community is a national employment asset and something to be utilised to its best effect.

Our plan is to be at the forefront of that change. To be a shining example of how Small to Medium Enterprises (SMEs) can make a huge difference to the lives of those who have been injured. Not only by employment, but by advocacy and creating awareness of the problems many now face. We need to help and facilitate the way in which government, charities and industry communicate with the end vision of ensuring all service leavers have the opportunity for meaningful employment.

In the words of Theodore Roosevelt:

"A man who is good enough to shed his blood for the country is good enough to be given a square deal afterwards".

THE ARMED FORCES COVENANT AND THE ORGANISATIONS WHO SIGN IT

The Armed Forces Covenant and the organisations who sign it

The future is bright for veterans, reservists, spouses and partners of those that are still serving. With the Armed Forces Covenant going from strength to strength, there has never been a better time to become a forces friendly employer or to seek one out. As this goes to print, over 3000 organisations, companies and charities have signed their covenant and momentum is growing. But more needs to be done.

Bigger companies can change hundreds of lives with one policy change, tweet or video from the CEO stating a commitment to veterans. Even an open letter in support of military spouse recruitment might be all it takes to create a supportive and safe environment.

How you can get Involved

To see how you can make a difference, just visit armedforcescovenant.gov.uk or search Armed Forces Covenant. From there you will find lots of information around creating a pledge to the nation.

Here are just some of the reasons why becoming a forces friendly organisation is good for business:

1   **Grow your network:** We have had some amazing opportunities to network with companies, charities and local authorities, we would otherwise never have met. Personally, I have created friendships, gained mentors and added business connections, just by getting involved with events. Of course, you need to be proactive. Initially, I attended events. Then, over time, I earned the opportunity to speak at conferences and insight days.

2   **Find new ways to recruit:** Being an Armed Forces Covenant (AFC) signed small company helps me to recruit the right people for our company. We recruit directly from reservist centres (unorthodox but it works).

3   **Tap into top talent:** Our military community is a national asset with a pool of well-trained individuals who uphold values and standards as a given. Their talents range from leadership within hostile and stressful environments to specialist technical training, from electricians (skilled in working with equipment with high voltage) to logistics experts.

DECLASSIFIED
DOCUMENTING MILITARY STORIES

In 2018, we started Declassified – a podcast that would change more lives than we could ever have imagined.

But why did a pest control company start a podcast that had nothing, absolutely nothing, to do with pest control? Well, I'm sure by now you'll appreciate that we aren't just a pest control company. In fact, we're a vision-led company.

We started Combat Pest Control with one simple belief – we had to help injured service personnel. So publicising their stories, raising awareness of their injuries and inspiring others with their tales of personal growth, was really important to us.

The initial idea was to meet a former soldier friend in a pub or café and record a conversation using our smart phone. No intro. No agenda. Just a conversation about their story.

We bought some basic microphones. But something held us back from pushing on with it. Firstly, the responsibility of telling the stories was enormous – it had to be done right. Did we have the skills to do it justice? The fear of getting it wrong held us back.

We needed help.

DECLASSIFYING STIGMAS WITH A SIMPLE CONVERSATION

DECLASSIFIED
DOCUMENTING MILITARY STORIES

That help came from a chance meeting with our now good friend, James O'Brien, LBC presenter, journalist and great bloke. Des and I happened to bump into him at a Combat Stress supporters dinner in the Langham hotel. I'd been on his show several times before as a phone-in guest talking about small business, the London living wage and the difficulties facing military veterans and their families in the future.

The night passed and we exchanged twitter handles – as you do these days. I remember sending him a message saying that if he ever needed our help in any way then he could get in touch. He responded with something similar and I thought nothing of it.

A few months later, the podcast concept was still bobbing around in my head. So, I reached out and asked him for 10 minutes of his time to run over the basics.

Happily, he obliged. We met in Leicester Square after his show, one day in May. I'd been invited onto his show beforehand to discuss the issues we'd talked about. Afterwards, James; his producer, Beth Woodbridge, and me sat down for a coffee.

After I explained the idea of the podcast to them, we agreed the name needed to change (it was originally called 'The Squadron Bar').

Next, James gave me some sound advice on shaping the episodes:

1 Get great audio.

2 Plan your episodes and run a thread through the story.

And, best of all, Beth had also agreed to produce the first 2 conversations.

I went away with a lot to ponder. Then Des and I came up with the podcast vision:

By declassifying stigmas and perceptions we want to open up issues around mental fitness and wellbeing, talk in depth about subjects like post traumatic growth and delve into human development on a micro level. Our long term vision is to provide hope, guidance, support and help for individuals who are suffering from both mental and physical illness or injury.

Once we understood what we had to do, the name of our podcast was obvious – Declassified.

It's definition was perfect - to officially declare (information or documents) to be no longer secret.

DECLASSIFIED
DOCUMENTING MILITARY STORIES

EPISODE 1 - BRIAN WOOD MC

DECLASSIFIED
DOCUMENTING MILITARY STORIES

EPISODE 4 - DR WALTER BUSUTTIL

DECLASSIFIED
DOCUMENTING MILITARY STORIES

EPISODE 6 - LOUISE FETIGAN

DECLASSIFIED
DOCUMENTING MILITARY STORIES

EPISODE 7 - DEREK & MARIA HUNT

DECLASSIFIED
DOCUMENTING MILITARY STORIES

EPISODE 12 - DAVID WISEMAN

DECLASSIFIED
DOCUMENTING MILITARY STORIES

EPISODE 14 - LEVISON WOOD

As this goes to print, we have created 22 episodes, achieved 75,000 downloads and have covered topics including: post-traumatic stress disorder, depression, suicide, child carers, tolerance and acceptance, betrayal, mass-trauma, loss, child abuse, as well as domestic violence.

The topics are hard-hitting. But there are major positives to gain hope and inspiration from. Many of our guests have spoke about post-traumatic growth – that is the ability to develop and gain strength from a traumatic experience.

How is it possible that someone as horrendous as mass murder can enable people to become a better more well-rounded individual now? Episode 4 with world leading psychiatrist Dr Walter Busuttil explains how post traumatic growth can make us stronger.

Plus, David Wiseman, talks about his post-traumatic growth experience in Episode 12. He is an amazing man who has been to hell and back, yet today stands as a role model to me (and many others). Please check out his episode and book (Helmand to the Himalayas).

All the guests on our Declassified podcast are members of the military community. Their stories have connected with people in ways that I could never have imagined. In some cases, even saving lives.

The podcasts prove that listening to others and understanding you are not alone is often enough for someone to commit to a positive action like contacting a doctor or approaching one of many charities that help (further information can be found here – www.declassifiedpodcast.com).

The Declassified podcast is a Combat Pest Control project. But it couldn't have happened without collaboration with the following people:

- Our amazing guests – Brian Wood MC, Terry Brazier, Phil Campion, Dr Walter Busuttil, Simon Harmer, Louise Fetigan, Derek and Maria Hunt, Sean Jones MC, Jordan Wylie, Alexander Khan, David Wiseman, Charlie Martell, Richard Sharp, Levison Wood, Richard Mearns, Maria Butwell, Amanda Jones, James Cameron, Paul Watson, Tony Riddle, Gulwali Passarley and Chris Kelly.

- The team at HESCO, who really do believe what we believe, and have shown fantastic support.

- Steve Brennan, who helped us to create our wellness plan that works alongside our episodes.

- Mr Gresty who has been with us from the very start and provides all our graphics as well as designing this very book.

- James O'Brien for the initial conversation and the continued support.

Both myself and Des would like to thank the one person that pulls this all together, our producer and friend, Beth Woodbridge. Her guidance, competency and skill have been key. We couldn't have shared these stories without her.

My final thought to leave you with in this chapter is that this podcast is a great example of what interdependency can achieve. No one individual could have created this on their own. But by combining different skill sets and personalities, we managed to surpass all of our expectations and create something that has had immeasurable impact on people's lives – Declassifying Stigmas with a Simple Conversation.

THE GROWTH GENERATION

THE GROWTH GENERATION

The 'Growth Generation' is a phrase I coined to describe those who served on operations in Iraq and Afghanistan between 2001 and 2016.

During this time, an intense period of war took place. Those who fought endured prolonged spells of heavy fighting in risk areas, resulting in stress, pressure and trauma.

But that's not the whole story. These experiences have also spurred this generation to develop in ways that have had a profound effect on the people around them and the organisations they lead.

In the mainstream media, we often hear about the negatives of war and conflict. We rarely hear about the positives. But if you look carefully, there are inspirational stories of 'post traumatic growth' and 'post conflict growth' growth to be shared.

It is true that Iraq and Afghanistan has made a permanent dent on our society. It will be spoken, written and debated about for many decades and centuries to come. But what I also feel confident about is what the Growth Generation (those who served in conflict and grew as a result) can teach the rest of us.

They relate to 6 key topics: world view, strength, ability, acceptance, relationships and wellness. Let me explain:

World view – an individual's world view can be influenced by many factors including the country you were born in, religion, culture and also conflict. I see it time and time again: those who have experienced trauma, life-threatening risk and situations of prolonged stress, have developed a more relaxed and accepting world view. As long as individuals or organisations aren't impacting the happiness of others, their view is: live and let live.

Strength – many talk about finding strength that just wasn't there before the trauma. Maybe it's physical strength, which is often found in participants of the Invictus games. Or mental resilience, which comes from facing huge and previously daunting challenges like scaling mountains, public speaking or setting up a business. This 'I can survive' attitude makes other endeavours somewhat more attainable.

Ability – others find new abilities and skills through trauma and conflict. New situations demand new solutions and innovation takes place. For example, the medical advancement in blood transfusions, plastic surgery and prosthetics has been incredible. Looked at from another angle, the ability to seek help (and encourage others to do the same) means this generation are publicising issues, breaking down stigma and changing society for the better.

Acceptance – recently, a friend told me he had accepted the traumatic experiences that have happened to him. And how his acceptance was encouraging others to do the same. What I have found is that this Growth Generation are taking acceptance to another level. They are using it to positively impact others affected by conflict. Whether that is providing education to children, training local medics, fundraising or advocating peace, this community is achieving great things.

Relationships – spending time away from loved ones can naturally create issues and problems. Returning can be equally turbulent, especially when it comes to understanding what both parties have been through. But, those that have been through adversity, are showing signs of closer bonds with siblings, partners, children and friends. They also develop closer relationships with team mates in civilian life, which can result in happier and more productive departments and organisations. I personally have experienced this with several of the podcast guests. A close friendship has developed as a result of our conversations.

Wellness – understanding and managing your own body and mind is key to longterm wellness. I have learned some remarkable lessons from those around me. The most important of those is the need to have a metaphorical toolkit to help look after yourself. Everyone is different. And different people need different things. But it could be: physical exercise, avoiding alcohol, using breathing techniques, yoga, spending time in nature, reconnecting with family and understanding the importance of meaningful employment and really making your mark doing something you love. Many of my friends who have served on many operational tours are now seeking purpose and meaning to aid in their own longterm happiness and wellbeing.

Here's my take. The Growth Generation teaches us how to become a better, stronger, more accepting individual who seeks meaning, purpose and holds values above everything else. The ability to grow because of your traumatic experiences isn't limited to members of the military but extends to members of our emergency services, survivors or sexual abuse, PTSD sufferers and those who have overcome a plethora of traumatic experiences. However, our military community is a shining example and role model to all walks of life that the trauma isn't the end. It can be the beginning.

LEARNING TO LEAD WITH THE SEARCH METHOD

WAR AND PEST

USING THE SEARCH METHOD

What makes a successful team? Super star individuals who outperform the rest? A competitive environment which pushes everyone to be their best?

Not in my experience. With over 17 years protecting lives in the armed forces and the fire service, here's what I've learned.

Success comes from interdependency

During my career, I have seen the same pattern repeat itself. Teams that really succeed are not just made up of people who are extremely competent at what they do. They are made up of people who know how to blend together to achieve a greater goal.

When we look at organisations like the British Armed Forces, our Emergency services or charities and companies like STOLL housing, Combat Stress, B1G1, TOMs and many more, what we find is exactly the same - one team working together to achieve a mission that's bigger than themselves. And within those organisations lie other organisations. Supporting partners who contribute to the main objective, which is vital in the overall successful outcome.

The message and mission within separate organisations will almost always be different. But success in any endeavour is found by bringing together individuals that share the same set of core values to achieve a common objective.

Leading an interdependent culture

Whether you are leading a team, an organisation or working with other partners across a sector (such as social housing), you can create an interdependent culture which will help to achieve more than you thought possible.

This chapter will show you how.

USE THE SEARCH METHODOLOGY TO CREATE INTERDEPENDENCY:

Let's start with the SEARCH methodology. This is central to how Combat operates. And it's easy for you to adapt it to your team or organisation, too.

Below you'll find a quick overview of the principles. Then you can flick to each chapter for all the detail on each section.

Systems
We develop best practice ways of doing things that everyone follows. In our world this means working to clear guidelines, manuals, checklists and standard operating procedures.

Education
We share information and learn from mistakes. This creates trust and develops a community that is committed to helping each other.

Accountability
We clearly define roles and responsibilities, so everyone understands what part they play in the success of the team. We empower people within teams so that decisions are made quickly and competently.

Risk
We genuinely care for others in our team and put the interests of others first. This enables a culture of trust and cooperation to thrive.

Control
We empower members of the team to take control of a situation, using leadership, influence and best practice knowledge.

Help
We understand that nothing of any value can be achieved by yourself. To be part of something you have to give and receive help. When this is put into practice, interdependency thrives.

LEADERSHIP SYSTEM

Systems are an integral part of any high functioning team. From the All Blacks rugby union team to the British military and large global organisations like Ben & Jerrys or Patagonia. Implementing systems creates clarity, consistency and efficiency.

What is a system?

A system is a documented way to do something. Generally, a task that needs to be done again and again by multiple people. Put simply, it can be a set of step by step instructions that ensures the same task is done to the same standard, every time.

How to create a system

Start by identifying the key tasks your business carries out, then make a system document for each task.

1   Identify the aim – at the top of any system document the primary aim.
    Example: how to conduct a daily inspection of your company vehicle.

2   Define time frame and responsibility – alongside the aim, try to estimate the time the system will take to complete and what role will be accountable for completing the task.
    Example: Driver of the vehicle should take around 6 minutes to conduct daily inspection.

3   Set out the steps of the system – keep it simple (10 steps max). More than 10 steps? Split the system into part 1 and part 2.

Use check lists, tick box spread sheets, diagrams, photos, explainer videos
to set out the steps.

Example

STEP 1	Open car doors using key fob
STEP 2	Open and close all doors
STEP 3	Whilst walking round the vehicle visually inspect body work for damage
STEP 4	Walk round vehicle again check tyres for any defects
STEP 5	Turn engine on
STEP 6	Turn all signalling lights and headlights on
STEP 7	Inspect lights are working
STEP 8	Check mileage and record in log book
STEP 9	Sign off vehicle in log book (check log book system)

You can add a video, diagram etc to help explain further.

Want to find out more about creating successful systems?
The E-Myth by Michael Gerber is a great source of information.

LEADERSHIP EDUCATION

Once the system has been created, it must be tested, then shared with everyone who needs to use it. This is all part of the education step.

When it comes to testing, use someone who is fully competent. Test, innovate or change. Then repeat until both parties are happy.

Now it's time to get it out there.

This can be done in many ways including:

- A printed company manual.
- Generic software like Dropbox.
- Secure and safe video playing service like Vimeo.
- Specific off the shelf software like SweetProcess or Process Street.
- Develop your own management software.

Sometimes it's a good idea to use two or more ways to educate your team, as everyone learns differently and not all solutions will suit everyone.

Whichever method you choose, make sure it is safe and secure and not available in the public domain.

One more thing, once shared, keep your systems open to feedback for future improvements. These systems should be working documents. Oh, and remember – creating systems takes time and patience.

"Accountability is something that defines me as an individual.

It defines Combat Pest Control as a company. And it's a value that I implore you to take on board and commit to."

Michael Coates

LEADERSHIP ACCOUNTABILITY

I have found that accountability is key to creating and leading in an interdependent culture.

Becoming an accountable leader

Accountability starts at the top.

To instil accountability, follow these key steps:

1 **Build a company/team culture (vision/ethos).**

Sometimes I hear organisations, large and small, talk about company culture like it is a fad or a campaign to increase morale. But a culture is more than this. It is the DNA of a team. The fabric of who you are as an organisation.

Charities do it very well as they want to 'sell' their vision.

Take Combat Stress for example. Their purpose is to 'provide our life-changing treatment to veterans from every service and every conflict'. It's simple but it's something they standby each and every day.

Look at STOLL whose vision is to 'house and support vulnerable Veterans to live as independently as possible.' They provide affordable, high-quality housing and support services to over 600 people each year. Their work enables vulnerable and disabled Veterans to lead fulfilling, independent lives.

Creating a vision and continually sharing it, in newsletters, videos, internal mail, external marketing, is vital to your company's identity. It explains who you are, what makes you different, what you are doing right now and where you are going in the future.

Once you are clear on what your vision is, make it your mission to share it with every team member, regardless of what job they do.

Like values, vision is something that existing and new team members should naturally align with. A shared vision, shared values and a shared sense of belonging creates a strong interdependent team and an organisation that's moving forward together.

- **Identify your values**

A value system is a set of principles that drives ethical action and decision making. Put simply, it's who you are and how you act.

Values are subjective. That means you can choose the principles that matter to you. Recruit your team and choose your suppliers based on who aligns best with your values.

Document them, share them and act on them. Living by your values defines you.

For example:
Imagine one of your values is integrity.

You are leaving the office at 3 o'clock in the afternoon. In full view of everyone, you notice a discarded food wrapper on the floor. You pick it up and place it in the waste bin even though this isn't your waste and your offices get cleaned twice daily. But, you have integrity and are living by your core values.

Now, similar situation, same discarded wrapper but the time is nearly midnight and you are the only one in the office, cleaner is coming in at 0600hrs. Do you pick it up or walk over the wrapper?

Like I said, values are subjective but integrity is integrity and those strong principles create accountability and build trust between team members.

- **Build trust**

Within a team, accountability builds trust like nothing else I have experienced. Knowing that the person to your left is going to conduct themselves and carry out the task to the T is reassuring and ensures you always hold yourself to the same standard.

Having clear Systems that are easily understood thanks to robust Education means that Accountability can flourish. Everyone knows what to do, how to do it and who's responsible for what. This in turn builds trust and creates high standards through working interdependently.

In my experience, I have found that team-building exercises rarely work. Instead, having individuals around you that believe and trust in their team, the company and its vision is much more motivating.

- **Invest in people**

Develop your team and make each one a better individual through working with you. Invest money into leadership and development courses and/or invest time into mentoring and coaching. Whichever you choose, investing in those around you will contribute to an accountable group.

• Know when to apologise

We are all human and in the generation of social media, strong leadership within an organisation or team sometimes requires humility and once again – living by your values.

This doesn't mean you're always wrong, or you have to apologise for everything that goes wrong, but admitting you have made a mistake and apologising to the team is essential in remaining an accountable leader. Next, it's important to come up with a way that ensures it won't happen again. So if you messed up with a VAT return, create a system that ensures you are never late filing and paying HMRC again. Job done.

• Leave 'the shirt' in a better place

This is the second time I have referred to the New Zealand rugby union team during this book but I love the way those players think. They're probably the greatest example of sporting interdependency you are likely to see. For them, it's all about the end objective. Regardless of who they are, or how good others think they are, they are only ever borrowing that shirt and number which is on their back. To that end their whole ethos is making sure the shirt is in a better place than when they initially borrowed it.

This can mean helping younger players, following and developing game systems (or calls) and generally living by what we are talking about in this book. Leave the shirt in a better place or leave your job role in a better place, you might not be there forever and what better example of accountability than know you did your best to enable this to happen.

LEADERSHIP RISK

What risks are you prepared to take to become a better leader?

This chapter will help you move from a manager of people (who puts their own needs before those of their team) to a leader of people (who puts the team before them self).

Whether you lead a large organisation, division, team or SME these points will help you improve as a leader, create a safe place for your team to thrive, and in turn enable an interdependent culture to prosper.

As a former soldier and fire fighter, I have many friends who have shown great courage on and off the battlefield and the fire ground. When asked why they did what they did, the answer is often the same: "They would do it for me".

Strong and capable leaders share this overwhelming feeling of selfless commitment and belief in the inert value of sacrificing yourself before your team.

An extreme case of this is our friend, and Declassified podcast guest, Sean Jones MC. His leadership under-fire against a very real and dangerous threat not only won him the military cross, but also ensured he didn't lose any of his men. By putting himself in harm's way, he showed great competency, trust for those around him, honesty, love and commitment. None of these alone can be put on a spread sheet but together they create something amazing.

True leadership is about never sacrificing others for your own gain, creating strong bonds of trust, responsibility and belonging and doing what you can to develop those around you.

With this in mind, here's our guide on how to lead, not manage:

Sacrifice

As I mentioned with Sean, strong leaders set an example, lead from the front and when the going gets tough, they make bold decisions in challenging situations.

Another friend of mine, Brian Wood MC, (appeared in Episode 1 of the podcast, his book – Double Crossed is incredible) showed another example of sacrifice and leadership. A former member of his Army battalion had fallen on hard times in the run up to Christmas. So Brian took it upon himself to assist his former teammate. He quickly set up a 'fundme' site, ran an impromptu marathon the next day (he had never ran this distance before and was generally speaking 'unfit'). In doing so, he inspired hundreds of people whilst raising over £3000 to assist this family in need.

Brian sacrificed his time and physical health to ensure someone else didn't have to worry in the short term. Great work, an inspirational act and a true leader.

So, NEVER sacrifice your team. Always set the standard. Be there to support them when times get hard. And be prepared to sacrifice yourself, so others may prosper.

Belonging

Work on creating a strong sense of belonging in your team. Resist the urge to get side tracked by factors that are outside your control. Use your vision and values as a compass in decision making, so you stay true to your purpose and protect the integrity of your company and its people.

Opportunity

When the time is right, raise those around you. Provide every opportunity for personal and professional development. Encourage education and build your team's self-confidence. Strong systems ensure that discipline is maintained. But by creating an environment which promotes growth, you'll also promote trust and increase loyalty. This method of looking after your team produces individuals that want to contribute by take the opportunity you provide.

Protection

Do everything you can to protect those around you and live by this moral value.

In the fire service I had great mentors and leaders. These guys would train me, test me, train me again and even if I messed up on a job they would protect me and would never let me down. The list of those individuals is long but Carl, Andy, Andy, Jeff, Rob, Sean, Ian, Kev and Toby are just a handful of them.

So do the same: train, develop, mentor, maintain, improve, support and protect.

Failure

Create a safe and secure team by teaching them not to be afraid to fail.

This doesn't mean setting them up to fail or allowing past mistakes to be repeated over and over again. Instead, it means not to be afraid to try new ways of working. This creates a culture of experimentation and innovation.

For example, you could invest £100 in running a social media ad campaign or create a professional training video series. The question is, will it kill the business if it fails? And if it does, could you innovate, tweak it and go again?

Obviously, don't go into a big 'new business' meeting with an untested pitch. But you could test the pitch on social media, learn from your results and make the original idea even stronger.

Test, test, test and, above all, let those around you understand that it can fail. But failure isn't failure, it's a test.

"I have not failed.
I've just found 10,000
ways that won't work."

Recruitment

This is simple. Allow competency to get candidates to the final interview stage, then choose your team based on shared values. Does the person sat across the table from me believe in our company's core values – honesty, integrity, humility etc.

As a vision and values led business, it's crucial that other people live the values. And recruiting for this means it's embedded right from day 1.

Left and Right

Do those around you believe what you believe? Does the person to your left and to your right have your back?

This brings me back to trust and cooperation, creating safety, protecting, ensure belonging, providing opportunity, allowing testing and never sacrifice anyone for self gain.

Race to the bottom

Decision-making is such a key part of leadership and it can, especially in business, be pressurised around money. Budgets, buying the cheapest product or service, undercutting the competition and constantly racing to the bottom to fulfil short-term gains are traits I often see in individuals and organisations who manage and not lead.

Racing to the bottom has been a term used to describe situations where certain demographics or organisations become exploited, often resulting in everyone becoming worse off.

We see this practice in our own industry when decision makers attempt to play companies off against each other for the cheapest possible price.

Instead of aiming to be the cheapest, aim to give your customers the best 'value for money'. This means seeking out enriching partnerships that are based on shared values, where you can bring added value – all of which creates a transaction you are both happy with.

By not racing to the bottom, you get the appropriate amount of time, materials, expertise, documentation, communication, problem solving, resilience, people and more to do the job.

It means finding the best people to work with, those that believe in the same things you do and those who understand their value and how they can provide you with whatever it is you need (and in many cases more).

Don't settle for mediocrity, whether it's the company who supply your tea bags or the law company who provide governance and policy. Invest in people. This shows others you lead from the front.

Work and live with people who choose values over value.

LEADERSHIP CONTROL

This chapter is about taking ownership of the aspects you can directly control that help boost your own performance and that of your team, which in turn helps to create an interdependent culture.

Let's look at the methodology so far. We have covered systems, education, accountability and risk. Now it's time for control.

If you implement and control the systems the team, organisation or partnership will function as well, if not better, as if you aren't there.

- Create the systems.
- Create an education platform that allows others to thrive and provides a platform for success.
- Ensure you create a culture of accountability.
- And never sacrifice any member of the team for self gain.

All of this can appear daunting and a million miles away from where you are right now. But, actually, it's closer than you think. To get there, you simply need to focus on yourself and control what's closest.

Starting here...

Wellbeing

Controlling your performance and setting an example to your team also requires self-care and compassion. Looking after your own wellbeing (emotionally and physically) is a great indicator that you live by values. Self-discipline is part of that.

Now, I'm not a performance coach. I've just observed, implemented and modified what I have seen from others that I've worked with. The 5 points that always reoccur when I see or experience productivity and drive are:

Movement - Performing regular physical fitness training. That could be as simple as walking the dog to having personal training sessions. Stay active and, if you need to, seek professional assistance.

Nature – Spend at least 1 hour (ideally 2.5) in nature per day. Take a walk before work. Eat your lunch in a park under a tree. Or cycle the scenic way to work, through a park, in a forest or by a river. Spending time connecting with nature improves our wellbeing – so get some exposure on a daily basis.

Play – Don't spend all your time working. Have fun away from the workplace. Obviously, you love your business or job, but time spent doing a hobby, sport etc enables clarity of thought amongst other things.

Family/friends – Spending quality time with your loved ones is invaluable. In the military, work can come before family – and this can be devastating. Learn from the mistakes I have seen and connect. Tip: when you're with family and friends be fully present. Turn off work emails, switch your phone to silent and enjoy the time fully.

Get out of your comfort zone – As crazy as this sounds, I would recommend controlled discomfort. Doing something you hate everyday promotes resilience and perspective. Cold showers are the perfect example. Take a daily cold shower starting at 30 seconds and building up (there's lots of science behind this practice, which suggests it improves your immune and nervous system and decreases stress levels. For more information, look into the Wim Hof method). Other examples could be a hard training session or publishing a daily blog that pushes you out of your 'comfort zone'. Very soon you will get comfortable being uncomfortable.

Planning

Basic and effective. Plan your goals and map out what needs to be achieved. This makes it easier to ensure the aims and objectives are met.

Create a 12 month goal – something big. Then break that down into specific 3 month chunks. Within that 3 month chunk, pinpoint 3 main tasks that contribute to the 12 month goal and work on these every day. It can be something small but all those small increments will soon add up. Remember to review goals on a weekly basis and effective planning is often conducted in a pair or accountability group.

A good friend of mine produces a national radio show. They have a group planning session every day, which is a perfect way to create a great show.

Myself and Des use a book called the 'self journal'. It ensures we stay accountable to our goals and really pushes us forward day-to-day.

Implementing the plan

Now you have a plan. It's time to crack on and implement it.

Have a clear framework you can work within, understand who is doing what and follow the flow.

As I write this today, I've just been asked by the country's leading care home to create a flow chart system to combat bedbugs. If followed, this plan will protect their residents every day.

Planning methods will always change. But the most important thing is to implement and not just sit on it.

Create, develop and follow through.

Environment and people

There's lots of research that suggests different people affect our behaviour in different ways. I'm no expert, but what I do know is that when my environment is positive, and the people around me challenge and inspire me, I perform significantly better.

So, look around you. Who are you spending time with? Are they positive and do they professionally challenge you in a constructive way? A way that improves something specific or the team as a whole.

Shared values and complementing competency is a great way to promote a high performing environment. Having a team (not always fully employed and can be freelance/contractors) that have different skills but are pushing in the right direction is a must.

Your brain

Understanding how your brain works, and how to control your emotions, is one of the most valuable steps you can take in establishing control and developing your leadership skills. It can help you make better decisions and communicate more effectively.

I wholeheartedly recommend you purchase Prof. Steve Peters best selling book 'The Chimp Paradox'. To write any more on the subject would do his work a serious injustice. But rest assured, knowing what part of the brain you are in, at any given time, will help you gain significant control and enable real empowerment. It'll also help you develop greater self awareness – which is the basis of all personal development.

LEADERSHIP HELP

The final and, in some ways, the most important part of creating interdependency is knowing how and when to ask for help. And being ready and willing to provide it to others.

Actively seeking help

Each of us is stronger, thanks to help we've received. You simply need to be wise enough to ask for it.

Take mentorship, for example. I have been lucky enough to have several exceptional business mentors over the last few years.

I reached out to each of them to ask for help. All gave advice freely and generously, but never asked for any form of payment in return.

The two that have had the biggest impact on me are Ant Chapman and Mark Seastron. Both fantastic people who not only believe in what Des and I wanted to achieve, but also shared similar values.

If you are thinking about your development, be self-aware. Where are your weaknesses? Who can help you develop those into strengths?

Great mentors don't need to spend that long with you to impact the way you work or conduct business but having the ability to run an idea past someone who has experience, can see things differently or may have a contact or a better way of working is invaluable.

There are many ways to contact people who could help you.

- Your current network – you might have someone in the business already who you respect and admire, you may already spent time with an individual at a networking or community events.

- Potential network – LinkedIn and other social networking sites are a great way to find the right people to help you and, in many cases, you can help them.

Alongside mentors are trusted friends and workmates. These are the people who will give it to you straight and look out for you no-matter what.

I have this with Des. He's not just a friend, but my business partner also

I've spent a lot of time with him. We deployed to Iraq together twice. A lot of what I know and talk about in this section of the book is down to how we work together. It's not always perfect (sometimes it's far from it) but when you have individuals who you trust more than anyone, you can move forward.

Finally, don't be shy in seeking help from external suppliers/contractors and creating partnerships that work for you both. We only choose partners who share our values and find this alignment brings out the best in both companies. It's important to review your current suppliers, too. Retain those who share your business or personal values and get rid of others that don't.

Actively provide help

In an interdependent culture, help works two ways. So how can you help others?

Be the kind of person you want people to be around and make time to develop others. It's not hard and it can create amazing opportunities.

Could you mentor a junior member of the team? Instead of criticising, be there to bat ideas and point in the right direction when needed.

If someone asks for help, always respond even if you can't provide the support or guidance they need. By replying you'll also promote trust and generate good feeling.

And finally, help others you may never meet. Try to impact the world in a positive way on a regular basis. Enough micro impacts eventually develop into a crater. You could coach a local sports team, volunteer or integrate collaboration into your business or team. It's easier to do than you think.

HOW TO COMBAT PESTS USING THE SEARCH METHOD

As a business, it's our job to combat pests. So why are we teaching you how to prevent infestations? It comes down to this. The number of pests in our neighbourhoods is rising. But council budgets are falling. There are fewer resources available to eradicate the problem. We know that not every family can afford to use a private pest control company. But we believe that everyone should have the right to live in a pest-free environment.

We also strongly believe in residents, neighbours, housing associations and communities working together, interdependently, to tackle issues collectively. Success has a greater chance of being achieved when everyone is working towards the same goal, using the same system and methodology.

In the next chapter, we'll share our system and methodology, so you can combat pests yourself.

Here's how we apply the SEARCH method to pest control:

S ystem – 6 simple steps to tackle the pest problem

E ducation – all you need to know about the pest on your premises

A ccountability – a run down of who should do what (and when to call the professionals)

R isk – an outline of the risks to be aware of

H elp – how to get help if you need it

We've focused on the most common urban pests that pose a risk to our health. There's also a chapter on less common household pests that cause anxiety, but don't pose a health risk, like silverfish and biscuit beetles. Plus, if you run a business that handles food (for example, a grocery shop, takeaway, café or restaurant), you'll find the section on food handling useful.

When combating pests, there are a number of risks involved – whether that's the chemicals you use or the risk of disease that pests can spread. We'll make these clear as we go along. We'll also point out when you'll need a professional pest controller's help (either from the council or a pest control company, like ours).

We'll give you all the help you need to understand the pest you're dealing with. And tell you what you need to know to stay pest-free in the future.

By the end, you'll be armed and ready to deal with whatever pest comes your way.

SYSTEM

Creating a system is the initial step in creating and maintaining a pest-free environment.

In our system, there are 6 steps:

1   Preparation and reconnaissance (what's the environment like?)

2   Identify (which pest you have)

3   Plan the treatment (how to get rid of it)

4   Implement the plan (carrying out the work)

5   Confirm the plan has worked

6   Reorganisation and further monitoring (future checks)

Step 1: Preparation and Reconnaissance

Start the pest control process with a survey or 'recce'. It's time to see your home or premises through the eyes of the pest. How would the pest have entered your home? What is it eating and drinking? Where is it living/nesting?

Preparation

- Spend time recognising and understanding potential risk areas such as entry points, food supplies, water sources and harbourages (where the pest lives).

- You can use the information in the rest of the book to help you take steps to prevent pests making your home their home (by putting in place improved cleaning systems, blocking entry points, removing food sources etc).

Reconnaissance

Following your recce, it's time to work out what you'll need to tackle the issue.

Let's use a domestic kitchen as an example:

- Be thorough in your recce/inspection highlighting possible areas of entry (around pipe work) and other structural issues.

- Work out how to access those areas. Do you need to move large or heavy objects? Will you need personal protective equipment like gloves? Are there electrical appliances in the area?

This can be done visually if you are conducting works yourself or logged in a treatment survey or report under observations.

The more you know, the easier the task, and as the old Army 7 P's adage goes:

- Proper Planning and Preparation Prevents P**s Poor Performance.

Step 2: Identify (which pest you have)

It is possible to prevent pests inviting themselves into your home and onto your premises. If it's a home, this not only protects your loved ones and family, it protects your property. If you're a business, it protects public health and helps maintain your reputation.

Start here...

Education – take steps to understand the pest you're dealing with. Read the Education section of the book (p70-111) to find out how you can make your home uninhabitable for pests.

History – has the area suffered a pest infestation in the past? If the answer is yes, this will give you clues to what problems you could face in the future. Check out the Control chapter (p124-135) for more information.

Adjacent Properties – are there issues with how people are living or how businesses are operating near to your property or land?

Future plans – are there structural or drainage works planned? Is there going to be renovation work close to were I live? How will this effect the current situation and what pests could this attract or 'unleash' (especially when drainage/sewage is being worked on or around).

Step 3: Plan the treatment

Now it's time to plan the treatment.

Whether you are planning preventative measures such as rodent proofing or actually trapping a pest, understanding the basics is vital.

Begin by thinking about:

Equipment – including safety kit, waste removal tools, hand and power tools. If you have a current infestation and require trapping, baiting, spraying etc, our advice is to seek professional assistance.

Professional – if you need a professional, who will you ask? Always find a reputable organisation who are accredited. In the case of pest control look at those vetted by either the NPTA/BPCA and WHICH trusted trader (this can also be a great way to find other trades and services).

Depending on the pest issue, you may need a pest controller who can manage CCTV of drainage, waste removal/disposal, building work, working at height access etc.

Timings – how long will it take and how many visits will you need? A simple example is proofing a property against mice. This will need at least two separate visits. One to initially clean, clear and proof the area. Plus, a second visit to confirm it has worked. As a rough estimate, proofing a property can take more than 4 hours. A confirmation visit takes around 40 minutes. Don't rush (remember the 7 Ps).

Step 4: Implement the plan

Time to actually do the work!

By this stage you should have ascertained several aspects of the work so far.

Write these down in a treatment report:

- **Target species** – Rats, mice, bedbugs...

- **Observations** – What, how, why...

- **Health and Safety considerations** – Protective equipment, manual handling, safe use of tools...

- **Actions** – What you have done.

- **Treatment** – What are you going to use and in the case of professional pesticides what products including HSE numbers when applicable.

- **Map** – Create a map of the area explaining your actions with a simple key.

- **Specific recommendations** – Such things could include remedial work and/or long term factors that need addressing.

- **Notes** – Any other further details especially notes that you may need during a follow up/after care visit.

Finally, if you have arranged for professionals to complete the job, you should be presented with the above details for you to review and ask questions if needed.

Step 5: Confirm the plan has worked

Ensuring the work has been successful is a must. Regardless of what you have done or what a professional has completed, some after care is essential.

Example: Proofing a domestic property against mice.

The pest control work might take 5 hours to complete initially. But without confirming it has worked, this will be a waste of time. Be proactive with this one:

- Simply leave a small amount of food (example 5g of chocolate spread) on a paper plate in an area that has been proofed.

- If the bait stays, perfect. The proofing has been a success.

- If the bait goes revert back to step 1 and start again.

Step 6: Reorganisation (and further monitoring)

Time to relax and go home for tea and a medal. Or is it?

The reorganisation process is just as integral as any of the previous 5 steps. Simply put, what will you do differently from now on to make sure the pest problem doesn't reoccur?

Basic stuff: keep on top of your housekeeping, in your business or at home. Make sure you are regularly checking areas prone to pest activity and identify any other high risk areas of the home.

The 'reorg' can also be a good time to restock equipment used and also a time for reflection. What systems can we change to make sure this doesn't happen again? Can I educate my team or my family about how to do things differently so we don't have this problem again?

EDUCATION

This section is designed to help you understand the pest you're dealing with. Once you understand its habits, breeding pattern and what it needs to survive; you can start taking proactive measures to prevent infestations occurring.

COMBAT
PEST CONTROL

RAT - COMMON, BROWN, SEWER

An all too common pest that can strike fear, anxiety and stress into individual households and organisations throughout the world. May carry disease.

Who can do it?

Any non-professional.

How long it takes

4-5 hours, spread over several weeks.

What you need

- Disposable gloves
- Torch
- Flathead screwdriver
- Philips screwdriver
- BAIT

The results

Manage current rat infestations, prevent future ones and safeguard your property if an infestation is active.

There are two main types of rat: the Ship Rat and the Brown Rat (also known as the Norway, Sewer or Common Rat).

Ship Rats live near Docklands. But the most common type of rat in our towns and cities is the Brown Rat. These creatures are not indigenous to the UK. They came from Siberia and Northern China in the 18th century. They often live wherever there's waste to scavenge from and drains to live in.

How to spot a Brown Rat

- Blunt nose and muzzle
- Small eyes and ears
- Body length: 25cm long
- Tail length: 17cm
- Weighs 250-700g

Habits of a Brown Rat

- Brown Rats navigate by using their sense of touch. They use whiskers and body hairs to feel their way around an environment. They use this sensory information to memorise routes to food sources and entry and exit points to their burrow.

- They are nocturnal, so you'll often see them at sunrise and sunset. If they appear in the day, it's because they have found a plentiful food source. This is key to remember when identifying the infestation and what's triggering it.

- Brown Rats use their sense of taste to work out what is edible (can be eaten) and what is palatable (what they enjoy eating). They will often chew food and spit out the unpalatable parts. This is important to remember when checking the bait that you've laid.

- They have a highly developed sense of smell. They can use this to identify individuals, other groups and different rat species. They also use urination as a means of communication.

- Like mice, rats have an acute sense of hearing. Sudden, sharp noises will send them scurrying back to a safe place. They also use squeaks, like ultrasound, to communicate – alerting others nearby to potential danger. If you have a particularly bad infestation, you'll find that if one squeaks, they'll all run at the same time.

- Sight is a rat's least developed sense – they mainly use this to differentiate between light and dark.

- Rats will use their incisors to gnaw in order to get to food. So keep your eyes peeled for teeth marks in your environment.

Where they live

- Brown Rats live in burrows, close to their food source. The key is to identify the food source (including fresh water) then you'll find the burrow. Perhaps you're storing a big bag of grain or dog food outside. Or perhaps your food waste isn't sealed and rats are feasting on your leftovers.

- In urban, built-up areas, look for places that pests can hide, take up shelter and reproduce like cardboard boxes, piles of rubbish or waste bins.

- If it's a loft, the burrow may be in cavity walls.

- If it's a garden, it may be in a hedgerow. Look for a hole that's around 10cm in diameter. If it's well established, there may be several entry and exit points.

How they move

- Rats are skilled climbers, jumpers and swimmers. They can climb rough surfaces, vertical pipes and even get inside pipes if the circumference is no bigger than 10cm. They can jump 70-75cm vertically and over a metre horizontally.

- When it comes to moving, rats stick to the outskirts: hedgerows, edges of buildings, along the foot of walls. They stay as close to their food source as possible and have regular patterns of movement. Though, in some cases, they can travel up to 30m radius. So when you do your checks, make sure you are checking for food sources up to 30m away.

Rats are neophobic

- This means they fear new objects, which is particularly important to remember when laying traps or bait. Any disturbance to their habitat will be viewed with suspicion.

- It can take hours, days or even weeks for a rat to get over a neophobic reaction to a new object. That's why, in some cases, we advise you to pre-bait an area. Put a trap or bait station near the burrow that's not pre-set. Wait some time (up to a week in some cases) then lay the bait.

- Try to disturb the environment as little as possible. Pre-baiting takes time and requires patience.

What they eat

Rats are omnivorous.

They eat:

- Grains, breads, vegetables, fats (especially near fast food restaurants) and food waste. If you do store food outdoors (like dog food etc), seal it in plastic boxes. And store food waste in sealed recycling bins, which are kept clean and tidy.

- Dog faeces and even the contents of the sewers in which they live. That's why having a Brown Rat in your food area, eating your food, is such a risk to your family or your residents' health.

- Water – rats need water to survive. So remove sources of free-standing water like: water in buckets, bird feeders or birdbaths. These are an ideal water source for the Brown Rat. If you have a leaking tap or any kind of pooling water, get these fixed and it will help to deter and finally eradicate the issue.

- Rats eat 10% of their body weight daily – that's about 20-30g of dry food a day. They gorge on available food and hoard it in their burrows. This is important to remember when it comes to choosing bait – you'll want to choose bait that's easily transportable, so the rat can take it back to its burrow and continue eating it there.

- Bait – when it comes to bait, there's plenty of choice on offer. Baits come as blocks right the way down to softer kind of paste baits. I recommend trying 2-3 different formulations or types to work out what the rat will respond to.

How many rats might there be?

- A colony starts with one pregnant female and grows to up to 8-11 rats.

- The highest ranking rats in the colony live closest to the food source. As the colony grows, more and more rats get pushed out to the periphery.

- They can change the location of their burrow. So when you are laying bait or traps, bear this in mind. If you haven't seen them in a week, they may have set up a secondary burrow – usually within 30m of the original one.

How they breed

- Rats are able to reproduce once they reach 12 weeks old.

- Gestation lasts 22 days.

- Rats have 6-11 in a litter.

- Once the babies are born, their mother will wean them for 22 days, but within that time she could become pregnant again with another litter – and so it goes on. In this way, it's easy to see that you could have an infestation of up to 50 rats in just a few months.

How to spot you've got a rat problem

- **Sightings** – if you've spotted a rat (or many rats), you'll know you have an issue.

- **Smell** – a stale smell, especially in confined spaces. For example, it could be in your loft or a cupboard in your home. Some people would say it smells like a sewer, but it's a real mix It's not a pleasant smell at all.

- **Droppings** – rat droppings are about 1.2cm. They can produce up to 40 a day. Fresh droppings will appear very shiny, especially if there's a water source they can drink from nearby.

- **Runs** – if the rats are outside, you'll get runs in the garden. These are a line in the grass or a line in the undergrowth where the rats are constantly moving between their burrow and the food source, or their burrow and a water source. If it's inside, you'll see smear marks – dark coloured smears which look like a black stain – where the rats are going in and out of a certain area, generally around a hole, or a gap, or a beam. That's caused by the underbelly of the rat brushing against it regularly.

- **Drains** – if there are signs of a rat leading into drainage areas or sewers, it's likely the burrows are underground. An extremely high percentage of domestic infestations stem from faulty, broken, and or substandard drain systems.

- **Electrical wires** – look out for signs of gnawed and exposed electrical wiring, especially in loft or attic areas. If you do come across this, you should look at isolating this part of the electric system – as it can pose a fire risk.

HOUSE MOUSE

A tiny pest, capable of huge amounts of destruction. Commonly found in and around where food is stored. Can carry disease.

Mice have lived among humans for thousands of years. This chapter deals mainly with house mice, but the same procedure can be used for field mice and yellow-necked mice. They build nests near food sources, and as these are often in kitchens or food stores, pose an added risk to human health because of their ability to spread disease and pathogens over every surface they move across.

How to spot a House Mouse

- Grey or brown fur, with a lighter coloured underbelly
- Small eyes and ears
- Body length: 7-9cm long
- Tail length: 7-9cm
- Weighs: 18g

Habits of a House Mouse

- Like rats, mice navigate by using their sense of touch. They use whiskers and body hairs to feel their way around an environment. They use this sensory information to memorise routes to food sources and entry and exit points to their burrow.

- Like humans, mice can recognise the following tastes: sweet, sour, salt and bitter. Though what they prefer to eat differs from one area to the next.

- They have a highly developed sense of smell. They can identify individuals, other groups and potential partners by smell. They use urination as a means of communication. It is a misconception that they have weak bladders. In fact, they have great control over their urinary movements, using it with sniper-like accuracy to mark and maintain their territory.

- Mice have an acute sense of hearing. Sudden, sharp noises will send them scurrying back to a safe place. They also use squeaks, like ultrasound, to communicate – alerting others nearby to potential danger. Mice also use their hearing to detect the approach of predators.

- Sight is a mouse's least developed sense – they mainly use this to differentiate between light and dark. They mainly stick to dark locations, for safety.

- Mice will use their incisors to gnaw in order to get to food. So keep your eyes peeled for teeth marks in your environment.

Where they live

- Mice live in nests anywhere in the home that's warm, dry and has limitless access to a food source. Common locations include cavity walls, under floorboards, behind white goods appliances (like fridges, washing machines, dishwashers etc) or in store cupboards that are unkempt.

How they move

- Mice are adept at climbing and jumping.
- Characteristically, mice move with their underbelly very close to the ground.
- The largest part of their body is the head, so if their skull can squeeze through a crack, the rest of their body can fit too.

Mice are neophobic

- This means they are suspicious of new objects. This is particularly important to remember when laying traps or bait.
- However, unlike a rat, a mouse will investigate the new object quite quickly, then move on.

What they eat

Mice are omnivorous.

They eat:

- Grains, breads, vegetables, fats (especially near fast food restaurants) and food waste. If you do store food outdoors (like dog food etc), seal it in plastic boxes. And store food waste in sealed recycling bins, which are kept clean and tidy.
- Unlike rats, mice don't need fresh water to survive.
- 10% of their body weight daily – that's about 3g of food a day.
- Little and often – mice feed in small, sporadic sessions. In some cases, over 100 times a night!
- Bait – when it comes to bait, there's plenty of choice on offer. Baits come as blocks right the way down to softer kind of paste baits. I recommend trying 2-3 different formulations or types to work out what the mouse will respond to.

How many mice might there be?

- There can be up to 12 mice in one colony. A colony will have one dominant male who deters all other subordinate males from breeding with his females.

How they breed

- Mice are able to reproduce once they reach 5 weeks old.
- Gestation lasts 20 days.
- Mice have 5-8 in a litter.
- Once the babies are born, their mother will wean them for 22 days, but within that time she could become pregnant again with another litter – and so it goes on. In this way, it's easy to see that you could have an infestation of up to 2000 mice per year (in perfect breeding conditions).

How to spot you've got a mouse problem

- **Sightings** – if you've spotted a live or dead mouse, you'll know you have an issue.
- **Smell** – in particularly large mice infestations, you'll find a stale smell. Especially if it's in a confined space.
- **Droppings** – mouse droppings are about 3-7mm long.
- **Gnawing** – mice continually gnaw in search of food. So look out for teeth marks caused by nibbling incisors.
- **Electrical wires** – one side effect of having mice in your home is the damage their gnawing does to electrical wiring, especially in loft or attic areas. If you do come across this, you should look at isolating this part of the electric system – as it can pose a fire risk.

CLOTHES MOTH

A proper nuisance when it comes to your wardrobe, carpets and upholstery. It likes nothing more than to chomp its way through your woollens, silks, upholstery and more.

Although the adult clothes moth is often the first sign of an infestation, it is actually the larvae that do all the damage. By the time clothes moths are fully-fledged adults, they no longer have the ability to feed on fabric.

How to spot a Clothes Moth

- A small straw or golden coloured moth, with no pattern on the wings.
- Wing span: 4-7mm long
- Eggs are tiny white balls, which stick to surfaces like glue.
- Larvae look like tiny white caterpillars: 2-3mm long. They build a web-like tent to live in. This can look like a silk, smooth line.

Lifecycle of a Clothes Moth

To combat Clothes Moths, it's important to understand their lifecycle.

- Simply put, they move from: egg, larvae, pupae, adult.
- Clothes Moths lay between 30-200 small white eggs in clusters.
- Eggs take 1-5 weeks to hatch, in temperatures of 10C and above.

- Larvae stay at that stage, feeding on your fabrics, for 2-7 months. This is when they are most destructive.
- Then they spin a tiny cocoon and get set to become a fully-fledged adult moth – this is called the pupa stage. They stay in the cocoon for anywhere between 2 weeks and 2 months.
- As an adult moth, they only live a few days or weeks. They no longer need to feed (all feeding is done at the larvae stage). Their primary focus is to find a mate and start the breeding cycle again. They die soon after.

What they eat

- Moths eat any kind of fabric derived from animals: wool, silk, fur, feathers.

Where they live

Clothes Moths live among fabrics where they won't be disturbed. So check:

- Under beds – where there's woollen or woven carpet to feed on. Or perhaps where you store seasonal clothes.
- Back of wardrobe – wherever you store your winter clothes or clothes you don't wear that often.

- Chest of drawers – the places where you store your woollen jumpers.

- Near skirting boards – some moths live near or under skirting boards, close by wool rich carpets.

- Moths are drawn to human sweat.

How to spot you've got a Clothes Moth problem

- **Fabric damage** – bald patches in your carpet, holes in your jumpers, dresses, scarves and curtains.

- **Sightings** – adult moths perching on walls, carpets or in wardrobes and drawers.

- **Web-like tents** – you may spot the remnants of a clothes moth larvae's home among your cloths.

- **Eggs** – tiny white balls or dots stuck to your jumpers, scarves, carpet etc.

- **Pupa case** – you may spot the trace of the cocoon, or pupa case, stuck to your fabric. These are only a few millimetres long and so thin they look transparent.

BEDBUGS

Bedbugs are small blood-sucking creatures that live in the cracks and crevices in and around beds, and feast on us as we sleep. Bedbugs aren't dangerous and don't spread disease, but the bites can be itchy and painful and these uninvited guests can cause stress and anxiety when they infest our homes.

How to spot a Bedbug

- Adult Bedbugs are oval-shaped and often reddish brown. They appear flat when they're unfed and get a more elongated oval shape when they're well fed.
- Size: 6mm long.
- Eggs are tiny white balls.

Lifecycle of a Bedbug

To combat Bedbugs, it's good to understand their lifecycle.

- Simply put, they move from: egg, nymph, adult.
- Bedbugs lay between 4-5 small white eggs, which appear in straight lines clustered together. These are glued into places like cracks and crevices around the bed.
- Eggs take 6-10 days to hatch, in temperatures of 13C and above.
- Nymphs are lighter in colour, gradually darkening as they get older. As they feed and grow, they shed their skin (exoskeleton). This can happen 5 times before becoming an adult.
- As an adult bedbug, they can live up to a year – even without feeding.

What they eat

- Blood – Bedbugs are parasites that live on the blood of mammals.
- They mostly feast on humans, but can also feed on cats, dogs and rodents.
- They feed nightly or weekly – as often as the host is present. When they do feed, it's for 10 minutes at a time. During this time, they can actually double, triple or quadruple in size. Once they've finished feeding, they'll creep back to a hidden crevice to wait until the next feed.

Where they live

Bedbugs live in the crevices and joints of your mattress and furniture. To find them, you'll need to check:

- Headboards.
- Mattress seams.
- Divan beds – between the interconnecting beds.
- Slats of the bed.
- Behind the skirting board.
- Behind the wallpaper.

LIFECYCLE OF THE BED BUG

Egg (1mm long).

First Stage Larva
(1.5mm long) Takes a blood
meal then molts.

Second Stage Larva
(2mm long) Takes a blood
meal then molts.

Third Stage Larva
(2.5mm long) Takes a blood
meal then molts.

Fourth Stage Larva
(3mm long) Takes a blood
meal then molts.

Fifth Stage Larva
(4.5mm long) Takes a blood
meal then molts.

Adult (5.5mm long)
Takes repeated blood meals
over several weeks. Females
lay up to 5 eggs per day,
continuously.

Note Bed bugs take 3-10
minutes to complete feeding.

How to spot you've got a Bedbug problem

- **Sightings** – small bugs or tiny white eggs in the crevices of your mattress, headboard, divan bed etc.
- **Bites on your skin** – these are red blotches, often in a line, which are itchy.
- **Tiny black spots on your mattress** – this could be their dried excrement.
- **Mottled Bedbug shells** – also called exoskeletons. Bedbugs shed their skin as they grow.
- **Smell** – unpleasant musty smell in your bedroom.

FLEAS

Fleas are small wingless creatures that seek warm-blooded animals to feed on. Quite often, that's our pets. But occasionally, it can be us. To get rid of them, you need to thoroughly treat your home and your pet.

How to spot a Flea

- Adult Fleas are dark mahogany in colour.
- Size: 2mm long.
- Eggs are tiny white balls: 1mm in size.

Lifecycle of a Flea

To combat Fleas, it's good to understand their lifecycle.

- Simply put, they move from: egg, larvae, pupa, adult.
- Fleas lay around 1000 small white eggs. These are laid after the female has a blood meal. Eggs are laid in the fur of the host, then the eggs drop off into bedding or onto floors.
- Eggs take 3-7 days to hatch into larvae.
- Larvae pupate after 3-4 weeks. They form a cocoon and emerge as soon as they can feel the vibration of a host nearby (like your cat, dog or rodent). If there isn't a host nearby, for example, if a property is empty but the previous tenants had a flea infestation, these pupae will lie dormant for a period of months until a new host moves in.

What they eat

- Blood – adult fleas are parasites that live on the blood of mammals.
- They mostly feast on cats, dogs and rodents, but can feed on humans too.
- Larvae are not parasitic. They feed on the skin of the host and the faeces, or the droppings, of adult fleas.

Where they live

- Animal fur – eggs are commonly laid amongst the hairs of your pet.
- Pet bedding – they thrive in hot humid conditions, especially if the bedding is near a radiator.
- Carpets and floorboards (and cracks between boards).
- Upholstery – sofas, armchairs etc.
- Behind the skirting board.
- In dust, fluff anywhere in your home.

How to spot you've got a Flea problem

- **Excessive scratching and grooming** – this is particularly a sign of fleas in cats. Cats often get fleas around their head and neck.

- **Crusting on your dog's fur** – dogs often get fleas on their hind-quarters.

- **Sightings** – fleas or flea faeces in your animal's fur or bedding.

- **Bites on your ankles** – these are red blotches, which are itchy. If the bites are above your waist (upper body, arms, head or face), you may have human fleas or bedbugs.

COCKROACHES - ORIENTAL

There are two common types of Cockroaches in the UK: the Oriental Cockroach (larger) and the German Cockroach (smaller). This chapter deals with the Oriental Cockroach, which is found in hot but damp areas.

How to spot an Oriental Cockroach

- Oriental Cockroaches have a dark brown, or black, shiny body. They have an extremely flat appearance.
- Females have a wider body than males and appear as though they don't have wings.
- Males have long wings that cover two thirds of his abdomen.
- Neither sex can fly.
- Size of male: 18-30mm long.
- Size of female: 20-27mm.
- Eggs are laid in large egg cases (called oothecae)

Lifecycle of an Oriental Cockroach

To combat Oriental Cockroaches, it's good to understand their lifecycle.

- Simply put, they move from: egg, nymph, adult.
- Females carry up to 5 egg cases, each containing around 16 eggs. She will deposit these in different places. How she deposits them is important to understand – as this will help you control the infestation (we'll talk you through this in the Control section).

- Eggs take 6-12 weeks to hatch.
- Nymphs are smaller versions of the adults. They take a further 6-18 months to reach adulthood.
- As an adult cockroach, they can live up to 6 months.

What they eat

- Cockroaches are omnivores.
- They eat rubbish, food waste, decaying plant matter and anything you'll find in sewers.
- They need water to drink, but can survive if their food source has enough moisture.

Where they live

Oriental Cockroaches live in clusters in hot, humid places. They prefer dark spots. And only come out at night.

They can be found:

- In hotels.
- Multiple occupancy houses or flats.
- Laundrettes.
- Sewers or sink areas.
- Damp, dark environments like basements.

How to spot you've got an Oriental Cockroach problem

- **Sightings** – you'll see them scurry if you switch on a light in a dark room. Don't forget, these cockroaches are nocturnal and love a damp, dark place to live.

- **Smell** these cockroaches give off a strong, potent smell. This is used to communicate with each other.

COCKROACHES - GERMAN

There are two common types of Cockroaches in the UK: the Oriental Cockroach (larger) and the German Cockroach (smaller). This chapter deals with the German Cockroach, which helps itself to your food and leftovers.

How to spot a German Cockroach

- German Cockroaches are yellowy brown with black to brown stripes from behind the head to the base of the wings.
- Neither sex can fly.
- Size: 12-15mm long.
- Eggs are laid in large egg cases (called oothecae).

Lifecycle of a German Cockroach

To combat German Cockroaches, it's good to understand their lifecycle. This species is a prolific breeder. So once sighted, you must act quickly to combat them.

- Simply put, they move from: egg, nymph, adult.
- Unlike the Oriental Cockroach, which carries 5 egg cases at a time, the German Cockroach carries 1. But this 1 egg case contains 30-60 eggs. She carries these until just before they're ready to hatch. This will become crucial, when we get to the Control step. The female stays near her egg case. So wherever she is, the eggs are there too.
- Eggs take 2-4 weeks to hatch.
- Nymphs are smaller versions of the adults. They take a further 3 months to reach adulthood.
- As an adult cockroach, they can live up to 6 months.

What they eat

- Cockroaches are omnivores.
- German Cockroaches will eat almost anything (unlike Oriental Cockroaches who feast mainly on rubbish, waste and leftovers).
- They eat meats, sugars, starches and fatty foods. When food is scarce they even eat soap, glue and toothpaste. In famine, they turn carnivorous and eat each other's wings and legs.
- They need water to drink, but can survive if their food source has enough moisture.

Where they live

German Cockroaches live in clusters in hot places.

They can be found in:

- Hotels.
- Restaurants, cafés and fast food establishments.
- Multiple occupancy houses or flats.
- Kitchens, vents and air ducts.

How to spot you've got a German Cockroach problem

- **Sightings** – you'll see them scurry if you switch on a light in a dark room. Don't forget, these cockroaches are nocturnal and love to live near food.
- **Smell** – these cockroaches give off a strong, potent smell – especially when excited or frightened. This is used to communicate with each other.

WASPS

Can be a noisy nuisance in the garden and a major risk to public health if they nest in or around our homes.

How to spot a Wasp

For some people, it can be hard to spot the difference between a wasp, a bee and a hornet. This quick guide should help:

- Wasps have long thin bodies, brightly striped with bands of yellow and black. Bees are furry and vary in shades of black, brown and yellow. Hornets are slightly bigger than wasps and are chestnut brown and yellow.
- Wasp size: 12-18mm long.
- Bee size: between 8-20mm long.
- Hornet size: 20-30mm long.

Lifecycle of a Wasp

To combat Wasps, it's good to understand their lifecycle.

- Simply put, they move from: egg, larvae, pupa, adult.
- They live within an interdependent nest, where the workers feed the grubs.
- They develop into pupa in 4-5 weeks, which are fiercely guarded by the workers.
- Once the pupae is fully developed, they form adult workers.
- Early in the season, the workers are busy gathering food, bringing it back to the hive, feeding the young and building the nest. This is the best time to intervene before they become aggressive later in the season.

What they eat

- Rotting vegetation (like fallen fruit e.g. apples, plums, pears, berries).
- Sugary leftovers (like ice cream, lollypop wrappers, fizzy drink cans).
- Insects.

Where they live

Wasps live in a nest.

- They make a new nest every season.
- In Autumn, the new queens develop. They leave the old nest and set up satellite nests in warm, dry areas nearby.
- Ideal places for wasp nests are: loft spaces, cavity walls, structural cladding, flowerbeds and sheds.

How to spot you've got a Wasp problem

- **Sightings** – more wasps entering your home or foraging in outdoor areas, especially near bins and areas of fallen fruit.

ANTS - BLACK ANTS

Black ants are the most common type of ant in the UK. They live in our gardens and form an integral part of the ecosystem, mixing up our soil and making it more fertile. But when they invade our homes, it's time to take action.

There are thousands of species of ants, but the ones you're likely to meet most often are Black Ants, Red Ants (Fire ants) and, in some cases, Pharaoh Ants. We'll tell you about these in each chapter.

How to spot a Black Garden Ant

- Black Ant: 3-5mm long. Black in colour. They do not bite.
- Red Ant: 2-6mm long. They are deep red in colour and deliver a painful sting. This comes up as a white pustule, which feels like it's on fire – hence the name, Fire Ants.
- Pharaoh Ant: 2mm long. They are pale, straw, yellow with darker heads and abdomens.

Lifecycle of a Black Ant

To combat Black Ants, it's good to understand their lifecycle.

- Simply put, they move from: egg, larvae, pupa, adult.
- They live within an interdependent nest, with one queen (who can live up to 10 years) and between 5,000 and 15,000 workers (who live for around one month).
- All the eggs in the colony are laid by one queen. After 3 weeks the larvae become pupae. These are fiercely guarded and fed by the workers. 2 weeks later, they are fully grown workers.
- Once the pupae is fully developed, they form adult workers.
- The workers gather food, bring it back to the nest, feed the young and build the colony.
- In July, when new queens hatch, they double in size, grow wings and take to the sky to find a mate and start their own nest somewhere else. These are referred to as 'flying ants'. Many hundreds, even thousands, can be flying at one time. This can cause a lot of distress to households and we see lots of call outs about this.

What they eat

- Sweet or sugary food (plant nectar, rotting fruit).
- Sugary honeydew produced by aphids. They happily farm aphids, protecting them from predators, so they can feed off the substance aphids produce.
- Anything you leave on your food surfaces. They invade our homes in search of food to bring back to the nest and to feed the colony.

Where they live

Black Ants live in a nest.

- Ideal places for Black Ants nests are: under paving slabs, rocky areas, in soil (flowerbeds, lawns, plant pots, window boxes etc), in hollowed trees.

How to spot you've got a Black Ant problem

- **Sightings** – more Black Ants entering your home, especially on food surfaces and near bins.

ANTS - PHARAOH ANTS

Pharaoh Ants may be less common than Black or Red Ants. But if you spot them in your home, seek professional help straight away. That's because these ants live indoors and breed so quickly that an infestation can happen rapidly, which poses a real risk to you and your family's health. Read on to find out more about them.

How to spot a Pharaoh Ant

- Pharaoh Ant: 2mm long. They are pale, straw-yellow in colour, with darker heads and abdomens.
- Black Ant: 3-5mm long. Black in colour. They do not bite.
- Red Ant: 2-6mm long. They are deep red in colour and deliver a painful sting. This comes up as a white pustule, which feels like it's on fire – hence the name, Fire Ants.

Lifecycle of a Pharaoh Ant

To combat Pharaoh Ants, it's good to understand their lifecycle.

- Simply put, they move from: egg, larvae, pupa, adult.
- They take 5 weeks in total to develop into fully formed worker ants (3 weeks to develop as larvae and 2 weeks to pupate and become an adult).
- Pharaoh Ant colonies have many queens (unlike Black Ant colonies where there is only one). The queens are interchangeable, so the colony can survive indefinitely.
- Infestations happen extremely quickly because after breeding, groups of workers and queens leave the main nest and set up satellite nests. And so the cycle starts again.
- It's important to note that if the nest is disturbed, but not destroyed, this can make the infestation even worse. Once the Pharaoh Ants feel their nest is under attack, they bud (smaller groups slit off from the main nest) and form several new nests and the breeding cycle starts again.

What they eat

- Meat, cheese, fat, sugar, honey, jam.
- In hospitals, they feed on blood and intravenous diet fluids.
- Dead insects, mice and droppings can also provide a food source.

Where they live

Pharaoh Ants live in a nest.

- They are often found in residential blocks, hotels and hospitals.
- They make nests in the fabric of buildings (such as cavity walls, windows etc) or in plants and sterile supplies. They can spread through service ducts (like heating and electrical conduits). The ants forage for water around sinks and areas of condensation.
- They love hot, dry places – the ideal breeding condition is temperatures of 18-30C.

How to spot you've got a Pharaoh Ant problem

- **Sightings** – more Pharaoh Ants entering your home, especially on food surfaces and near bins.

FLIES - CLUSTER FLIES

Cluster Flies are a harmless type of fly, which live outdoors in summer, but can enter buildings (particularly loft spaces) to look for a place to spend the winter. Often, they enter en masse at the end of summer or early Autumn. Or appear on the window of little-used rooms.

How to spot a Cluster Fly:

- 7mm long.
- Distinct stripes behind the head. Short golden hairs on the thorax. Light and dark grey splotches on the abdomen.
- Slow moving.
- Part of the blowfly family (like bluebottles).

Lifecycle of a Cluster Fly

To combat Cluster Flies, it's good to understand their lifecycle.

- Simply put, they move from: egg, larvae, pupa, adult.
- Unlike Bluebottles, Cluster Flies do not lay their eggs in human food. They are strictly parasitic on earthworms.
- In summer, Cluster Flies lay their eggs near earthworm burrows and the larvae infest the worms.
- At the end of summer, they enter our homes to hibernate – often in large numbers.

What they eat

- Earthworms.

Where they live

- Fields – during summer
- Buildings – from late summer onwards. They will try to nest in roof spaces or in between roof felt and tiles or even behind wall cladding. They will emerge again in spring.

How to spot you've got a Cluster Fly problem

- Sightings – Cluster Flies can swarm into roof voids, so you may see or hear a large number in your loft or attic. There may also be sightings of dead flies on the loft floor.

FLIES - BLOW FLIES

Blow Flies are a family of flies that include Bluebottles and Greenbottles. They can cause a serious health risk through cross-contamination. That's because they lay their eggs in rotting carcasses, flesh and meat, then land on our food.

How to spot a Blow Fly

- Larvae: maggots are 18mm long, white like a grain of rice.
- Adults: 12mm long, deep metallic in colour (blue or green).

Lifecycle of a Blow Fly

To combat Blow Flies, it's good to understand their lifecycle

- Simply put, they move from: egg, larvae, pupa, adult.
- Female Blow Flies lay around 150-200 eggs in rotten meat, animal carcasses or rotten flesh.
- Eggs hatch in 8-24 hours, turning into larvae (known as maggots).
- Larvae will feed on the corpse or rotten flesh, then burrow into the ground to pupate, emerging as adults 7-14 days later.

What they eat

- Blow Flies eat rotting flesh, dead animals, rotten meat and faeces.

Where they live

- Larvae (maggots) live in rotting animal carcasses.
- If you are finding multiple adults in your home, it may be because a mouse or rat has died under your floorboards, in your chimney, behind your cupboard, in your loft or elsewhere.

How to spot you've got a Blow Fly problem

- **Sightings** – one or two Bluebottles or Greenbottles in your home may tell you that the carcass is nearby, possibly outside. Multiple Bluebottles or Greenbottles in your home may tell you that the carcass is in your home.

FLIES - FRUIT FLIES

Fruit Flies are pesky creatures, found in summer, hovering in your kitchen near your fruit bowl or around your bin. Like any fly, they pose a risk to health by cross-contaminating food surfaces with bacteria – causing diarrhoea and upset tummies.

How to spot a Fruit Fly

- Adults: 3mm long, light yellow to tan in colour.
- Fly erratically, close to their food source.

Lifecycle of a Fruit Fly

To combat Fruit Flies, it's good to understand their lifecycle.

- Simply put, they move from: egg, larvae, pupa, adult.
- Eggs are laid on the food source.
- Larvae emerge and feed on the surface of the food for 5-6 days.
- After this, they crawl to a drier part of the food source, or even out of the food source, to pupate 2 days later.
- Life cycle from egg to adult is around 10 days in total.

What they eat

- Overripe fruit and vegetables
- Fermenting materials, like leftover beer or soft drinks.
- Food waste in your recycling bin.

Where they live

- Fruit Flies lay their eggs upon their food source. They also attracted to anywhere moist, like wet rags, dishcloths and mops.
- Look for areas where fruit and vegetables are stored outside the refrigerator. This could be in a fruit bowl, on a work surface, in rubbish bins and around recycling bins.
- Even spilled juice under an appliance could be a breeding site.

How to spot you've got a Fruit Fly problem

- **Sightings** – multiple small fruit flies hovering near their breeding site and food source.

FLIES - SEWAGE FLIES

How to spot a Sewage Fly

- Adults: 2mm long, almond shape, hairy in appearance.

Lifecycle of a Sewage Fly

To combat Sewage Flies, it's good to understand their lifecycle.

- Simply put, they move from: egg, larvae, pupa, adult.
- Eggs are laid in the sludge found in sewerage works.

What they eat

- Bacteria and algae found in the sludge.

Where they live

- In or around sewage works
- In or around manholes, drains, septic tanks etc

How to spot you've got a Sewage Fly problem

- **Sightings** – multiple small sewage flies hovering near their breeding site.

SQUIRREL - GREY SQUIRREL

A mischievous garden dweller, who occasionally comes inside to nest in attics and roof spaces. They can do structural damage to your home and create a fire risk.

Grey squirrels were first introduced to the UK in the late 1800s. Since then, they have spread throughout England and Wales – to the detriment of our native species, the Red Squirrel.

How to spot a Grey Squirrel

- Grey or brown fur, with a lighter coloured underbelly.
- Small eyes and ears.
- Head and body length: 25-27cm long.
- Tail length: 20-22cm.
- Weighs 500g.
- Both sexes are a similar size.

Where they live

- Squirrels build their nest in several locations. Quite often they use forks in trees, very high up.
- Their nests are called dreys. They are used for shelter and breeding.
- Nests are a compact, spherical shape. They are slightly larger than a football and constructed of twigs, leaves, bark and grass.
- They stay close to their nest if food is abundant in that area. Otherwise they will forage further afield. Males will search up to 500m from the nest. Females will travel up to 250m away.

How they move

- Like other rodents, Grey Squirrels are agile climbers and jumpers.

What they eat

They eat:

- Fruit, nuts, fats (for example fat balls for the birds), seeds (especially bird seed).
- Acorns, bulbs, tree shoots, buds, fungi and roots.

How they breed

- Squirrels are able to reproduce once they reach 6-7 months old. But most reproduce when they are 10-12 months old.
- They have two litters a year. The first litter is born in February or March. The second is born in June or July.
- Squirrels have 1-7 in a litter.
- Once the babies are born, their mother will wean them at 8-10 weeks.

How to spot you've got a Squirrel problem

Squirrels in the garden are not necessarily a problem. It's when they enter your loft or other parts of your home that you need to act.

- **Sightings** – if you've spotted a squirrel in your home, you'll know you have an issue.
- **Noise** – if a squirrel has had a litter of baby squirrels in your loft, you may hear an increase in activity.
- **Droppings** – squirrel droppings are about 1.2cm long.
- **Gnawing** – squirrels continually gnaw. So look out for teeth marks caused by nibbling incisors.
- **Electrical wires** – one side effect of having squirrels in your home is the damage their gnawing does to electrical wiring, especially in loft or attic areas. If you do come across this, you should look at isolating this part of the electric system – as it can pose a fire risk.

FOXES

An integral part of the urban ecosystem. But can be a noisy nuisance from December to February. Foxes should be managed, not culled. We'll show you how to deter them from your garden.

How to spot a Fox

- Male and female foxes are similar in size and shape.
- Females have a slightly smaller skull and are slightly lighter in weight.
- Length: 65cm, head to body, reddish-brown and a white chest. 50cm, thick bushy tail (called a brush).
- Weight: up to 10kg.

Where they live

- **Foxes are territorial** – they move into any area that's unoccupied by another fox.
- **Foxes have several lairs and one or more breeding dens** within their territory.

What they eat

- Rats – foxes help control urban rat populations.
- Fruit, spiders, worms, insects, birds, carrion.
- Only 18% of their diet is made up of food waste (scavaging from our bins, ripping bin bags etc).

A year in the life of a fox

Foxes become a nuisance for short periods during the year. This is worth bearing in mind when faced with a fox problem. Often, the disturbance is short-lived and, with patience, it will cease in a matter of weeks. There are some steps you can take to make your home a less attractive place for foxes. We'll talk you through these in the Control section.

Late January – **Early February**	**Foxes mate** Vixens are only sexually active for 3 days during this spell. But they are noisy, finding a mate and eventually breeding.
Late February	**Find a den** Before giving birth, the foxes will find a safe den to have their litter. This could be under a shed, in a hedge, at the back of a garden.
March	**Vixen gives birth** There are up to 5 cubs in a litter. The male fox forages for food and returns to feed the vixen. The cubs feed from her milk.
April	**Cubs emerge from den. Adults moult** The vixen is still being fed by the male fox, but you may spot cubs in the garden for the first time. Adults lose their winter coat (called moulting). At this time, lots of people mistake this for mange. Don't worry, it's just the moult happening.
May	**Both adults hunting** By this stage, cubs are now eating solid food. So both adults hunt to feed them.
June	**The den is abandoned** The vixen has stopped producing milk. The cubs are 100% on solid food. The foxes may leave your garden.
July – August	**Cubs become more independent** Cubs forage for food themselves. Adults spend nights away from the cubs, as they begin to separate themselves.
September	**Cubs fully grown** They are indistinguishable from their parents, so it appears there are lots of adult foxes.
October	**Family group disperses** Cubs move on and find their own territories. Moult is complete in the adults.
November – **December**	**Fights over territory** Another noisy period as foxes fight over territory. Adults and subordinate adults fight as younger foxes find their own territory.

PIGEON - FERAL PIGEON

A common and widespread pest, which damages buildings and can carry disease.

How to spot a Feral Pigeon

- Plummage can be white, blue-ish purple or even black.
- Head and body length: 31-34cm long.
- Weighs 200g-600g.
- Both sexes are a similar size.

Where they live

- High rise buildings, balconies, tops of buildings.
- Nooks and crannies of derelict buildings, loft spaces, under bridges.
- Listed buildings or heritage sites, causing severe damage if left undisturbed.
- Nests are a crude structure, constructed of twigs, plastic, leaves, bark and grass. If nesting in lofts, they will use loft insulation too.
- Nests become saturated with droppings.
- They stay close to their nest if food is abundant in that area. Otherwise they will forage further afield. Males will search up to 500m from the nest. Females will travel up to 250m away.

What they eat

- Feral pigeons in urban areas scavenge for food, eating all types of food waste.
- They are prolific where food sources are abundant – near takeaways and restaurants.
- Some people feed pigeons in town centres, exacerbating the problem.
- Pigeons eat 30g of food a day and produce 2kg of droppings a year.

How they breed

- Breeding pairs have up to seven broods a year.
- There are two eggs in every brood.
- Main breeding times are March – July, when temperatures are favourable and food is plentiful.
- Eggs are incubated by both male and female birds for 17-19 days.
- Once hatched, young birds are fed by their parents for up to a month. After that, they become fully independent.

How to spot you've got a pigeon problem

- **Sightings** – an abundance of pigeons in a single area.
- **Noise** – pigeons make a soft cooing noise.
- **Droppings** – can be a slip hazard as well as a transmitter of disease.

Hazards of pigeons

1 **Building damage** – pigeon droppings are responsible for serious, and costly, damage in buildings.

- The droppings make the stone more porous, which leads to cracks forming. This is especially damaging to heritage buildings – and costly to repair.
- The droppings also damage metal and paint work.
- Lastly, droppings are laid in gutters and downpipes which may contain seeds. These seeds germinate, creating plants, which block the gutter very quickly. This leads to water damage inside the property which is costly to repair.
- Very soon, a beautiful building falls into disuse and disrepair, needing further cleaning, repairs etc.

2 **Spread of disease** – pigeons carry over 110 different pathogens, including 8 viruses and 55 fungi. These can be transmitted through droppings. If you have a large number of pigeons and a build up of droppings, this must be tackled as a priority.

3 **Secondary pest infestations** – pigeons can cause secondary pest infestations. That means they bring with them a multitude of other pests, like mites, spider beetles, book louse, mealworms etc.

4 **Health and safety** – pigeon droppings can cause a serious slip hazard, especially if they are roosting above walkways or staircases and entrances.

Law and the protection of pigeons

There is a lot of legislation around the management of pest birds like pigeons. This includes: the Protection of Animals Act, the Public Health Act, the Wildlife and Countryside Act, Firearms Acts, working at height regulations, to name but a few.

Secondly, the birds themselves are protected. So you need to a license to work near them or around them.

There are 3 types of license:

1 License to kill and take wild birds to prevent serious damage or disease.

2 License to kill and take wild birds to preserve public health and public safety.

3 License to kill and take certain birds trapped in food premises to preserve public health and public safety.

There is also strict legislation to follow around the proofing of buildings against wild birds.

For this reason, we recommend you contact your landlord or housing association to tackle the issue. They, in turn, need to use a licensed, professional, pest controller.

OTHER HOUSEHOLD PESTS

Other household pests come in all shapes and sizes. Some are harmful and need fast action, like the Common Furniture beetle (woodworm). Others are harmless, but can cause anxiety or distress, like spiders and dust mites. Here's how to deal with them.

Biscuit beetle

- Size: 2-3mm.
- Find them in your kitchen, wherever dried food is stored.
- Feeds on cereals, flour, bread, spices, seeds, beans, pasta, tea and other dried food. Can also be found in bags of dry dog food, bird seed or grass seed.
- They're tiny reddish-brown beetles, smaller than a poppy seed.
- You'll know you have an infestation if you see tiny pock-marked holes in food packaging. They eat through all types of cardboard, paper, foil and plastic film.
- Got an infestation? Here's how to treat it: trace the source of the infestation (it could be a bag of flour, a box of tea, a packet of spice). Once you've identified all the areas of infestation, dispose of infested food in outdoor bins. Vacuum and clean the cupboard/larder/food store thoroughly.
- To prevent or detect an infestation, use these control measures. Install pheromone-based traps or bait bags in food storage areas and check them regularly.

- If you own a café, take away or restaurant (or anything in the food handling industry), make sure you rotate stock regularly to alleviate any long-term risk of biscuit beetle taking hold within your food storage areas.

Common Furniture beetle (woodworm)

- Size: 2-5mm (adult).
- Adults are brown, wood-coloured, beetles with small dark heads and longer oval shaped bodies.
- Larvae are long, creamy white and C-shaped.
- Adults don't feed on wood. They only reproduce.
- Larvae do all the damage. They bore through wood to feed for 3-4 years.
- They feed on the starchy part of the wood – preferring sapwood.
- You'll find them in any area of your home that has wood. They invade structural timbers, furniture and other wood. They prefer unpolished, untreated wood, that's not smooth. So there's a little bit of unfinished area that the beetle can gain hold. The larvae can burrow in, and then the beetle will develop from there.

- Some building regulations state that you cannot use timber with more than 25% sapwood so that woodworm cannot substantially weaken structures.

- You'll know you have an infestation because you will see small, round exit holes of 1 to 1.5mm diameter. Active infestations have new exit holes and fine wood dust around the holes. This is where the larvae have burrowed nearer to the surface to pupate and emerge as adults, ready to reproduce again.

- Got an infestation? Here's what to do next.

  If it's a small infestation in your furniture, you can tackle it yourself with treatments bought in many stores. Just follow the instructions carefully.

  If it's a large infestation, or it's in the wooden structure of your home (for example, roof beams, floor joists etc), contact a professional pest company to thoroughly and rapidly treat the area. You will need to make sure that the pest company offer you a warranty on the treatment as it can take up to 4 years for larvae to develop as adults.

  If you are treating loft spaces, you must survey the area for bats first. Bats are a protected species. If you spot a roost, droppings or bat activity, you must contact your local nature conservation group to seek advice before tackling the woodworm issue.

Sawtoothed Grain beetle

- Size: 2.5-3.5mm.

- You're less likely to find these in your domestic kitchen and more likely to find them in a commercial kitchen, for example if you own a café, takeaway or restaurant (or any food handling business). They'll be in a food store, wherever dried food is stored.

- Feeds on grain, cereals, chocolate, pet foods and seeds.

- They're tiny dark brown beetles, smaller than a peppercorn.

- You'll know you have an infestation if you see mold growing on the food and the quantity of stored food getting smaller.

- Got an infestation? Here's how to treat it: trace the source of the infestation (it could be a bag of grain, nuts, dried fruit, pet food). Once you've identified all the areas of infestation, dispose of infested food in outdoor bins. Vacuum and clean the cupboard/larder/food store thoroughly.

- To prevent or detect an infestation, it's possible to use these control measures. Install pheromone-based traps or bait bags in food storage areas and check them regularly.

- If you own a café, take away or restaurant (or anything in the food handling industry), vacuum and clean the areas you store food regularly to control the risk of an infestation. Losing a large quantity of stored food can be costly to your business and pests can be a threat to your reputation.

OTHER HOUSEHOLD PESTS

House dust mite

- Size: 0.4mm (barely visible to the eye)
- Find them anywhere in your home.
- Feeds on dust created by flakes of human skin, animal skin and mold. House mites are not parasitic and don't burrow under our skin.
- Dust mites are not harmful themselves, but are associated with allergies in some people, causing wheezing and asthma. This can develop if, as a small baby, you inhaled the faecal excretion of dust mites when your immune system was not quite developed yet.
- It's very difficult to remove house dust mites completely. But it helps to keep on top of good hygiene. Follow these simple tips:
  - Vacuum mattresses and sofas regularly
  - Empty vacuum cleaners regularly
  - Wash bedding weekly
  - Use a complete mattress cover, wash every 2nd or 3rd month
  - Bedding with a threadcount of greater than 246 is less attractive to dust mites
  - Use a dehumidifier in summer. Dust mites prefer warm humid conditions, so keeping the humidity at less than 45% will help control them.

Spiders

We don't see spiders as pests, but we do understand the distress they can bring. So here are some tips to control them:

- Most spiders in this country are harmless.
- The media has escalated our fear around the presence of false widows. But here are the facts to help you correctly identify and avoid them. False widow spiders are 9-14mm in size with brown bulbous bodies and cream coloured markings similar to the shape of a skull. They can inflict a bite on humans, which is similar to a bee or wasp sting. False widow spiders do not usually bite unless they feel trapped or threatened. As with all kinds of wildlife, tread carefully.
- You can reduce the number of spiders in your home by following these top tips:
  1. Discourage flies – keep your food covered, clean your work surfaces after you've prepared food, keep sinks and drains clean and free from leftover food particles (which make tasty feasts for flies), keep windows and doors closed in summer or invest in fly screens, fly traps and insect spray (taking care to follow the instructions carefully). Less flies means less food for spiders, which quickly reduces the number that invade your home.
  2. Clean regularly – vacuum and dust thoroughly – especially areas that are hard to get to: under kitchen units, in the corners of a room, under the stairs, and high up in conservatory areas.

Woodlice

Woodlice are a common nuisance, but they do not damage your property or feed on your food or furnishings. They are a good indicator that you have damp areas in your home, which you should address.

- Size: 3-30mm long
- Hard grey shell with 14 jointed legs and 2 small antennae.
- Find them in damp areas of your home, as they search for moisture.
- They feed on dead plant material and they're usually active at night.
- To control them, remove their food source (dead plant leaves) and address damp areas of your home. Vacuum and clean regularly.

Snails and slugs (in your home)

- Snails and slugs can slither into your home in search of food. They have a great sense of smell and are attracted by pet food, kitchens or food stores.
- They squeeze through amazingly tiny cracks, under doors, through holes drilled for TV cables, gas or electricity and through air bricks.
- You'll know you have an infestation because you'll wake up to silvery slime trails over carpets, floors and even walls.
- To get rid of them, trace the slime trail back to their entry point, then seal any gaps using expanding foam for large gaps or silicone sealant for smaller cracks. Cover air bricks with a mesh or screen.

- Outside your home, remove any vegetation, grasses or weeds that's brushing against your walls.
- You'll soon stop them in their slithery tracks.

Silver fish

Silver fish are a primitive insect.

- Size: 18-22mm long.
- Silver/grey in colour.
- You'll find them in bathrooms and kitchens. They live in cracks and crevices behind tiles, wallpaper etc in the day and are active at night.
- You'll know you have an infestation as they'll scarper when you turn the light on at night. You may even see them move in the day.
- To control them, here's what to do:
  1. Thoroughly clean the area. You can use a residual insecticide, which is extremely effective.
  2. Seal cracks and crevices.
  3. Monitor the situation and repeat the steps above if you still have a problem.

FOOD HANDLING AND PEST CONTROL

Every business, organisation or charity that handles food must have a pest management programme in place. So whether you run a soup kitchen or a five star restaurant, you need to consider how you manage pests.

You can put your own pest management in place. If you're wondering where to start and what to do, this chapter will show you the basics.

Or you can ask a professional pest control company to help. At Combat Pest Control, we offer two different pest management programmes, which help you to meet the requirements set out by law and give you total peace of mind.

Here are the basics of pest management, using our SEARCH method.

Establish a system

1   Create a folder to document your programme.

2   Schedule 12 dates throughout the year, where you will do a pest survey.

3   During each survey, you need to check your establishment for pests, including food stores, preparation areas, waste areas and customer areas. All findings need to be documented. Create concise treatment reports to summarise what you've observed, any treatment you've carried out and what the recommendations are going forward.

Educate your staff

You are responsible for making sure your establishment is pest-free. But you can't do it on your own. You need to work together with your team to manage pests. That way, you can spot issues early before they become larger infestations that are a serious public health risk, costly to fix and damage your reputation.

1   Training should form part of every staff induction and should be refreshed regularly, so everyone understands the importance of managing pests and the associated risks to the public.

2   Educate your team on which pests to look out for. Install posters in key areas with identification information. They should be aware of types of pests as well as signs of pests (droppings, signs of gnawing, pock-marked holes in packaging etc).

3   Put in place working practices that everyone adheres to, which prevent pests invading in the first place. These are called proactive controls.

4   Make sure everyone knows how to report a pest sighting. Early detection and fast action can help avoid a costly infestation.

Be accountable

Food hygiene regulations, EC852/2004, lay down general hygiene requirements for all business operators, and state that the layout, design, and construction of food premises good food hygiene practices, including protection against contamination, and in particular pest control. They also state that adequate procedures should be in place to control pests.

Assess and manage risk

- Identify possible risks within the property: for example your location, the layout, the materials you're stocking.

- Categorize areas within your property as high, medium or low risk. Decide which pests may present themselves in each area of the property (food stores may attract mice, food preparation areas may attract flies, waste areas may attract rats)

- If you do need to tackle an infestation, and you decide to use bait, you'll need to use someone who is competent and knows how to comply with the strict legislation around this (Control of Substances Hazardous to Health or COSHH assessments). We would recommend using a professional pest controller for this. You'll need to document (in your folder) any rodenticide or insecticide used on your property and map areas this is being used. If this is required externally, you'll also need to do an environmental risk assessment, too. You also need to show how you are managing non-target species in these cases. A trained pest controller can manage all of this for you.

Use effective control measures

You can take steps to prevent pests from invading your food handling business. These are called proactive controls.

These include:

- Strict hygiene procedures.

- Good stock rotation.

- Responsible waste management.

- Installation of fly screens etc.

With regular inspections, and thorough staff training, any pest infestation should be detected early. You'll need to act quickly to eradicate it. That's because of the danger that infestations pose to public health. And because the longer you take to address it, the more the pest will multiply through breeding cycles.

- Bait, pesticides, insecticides and rodenticides need to be used in strict accordance with the law by a trained professional who completes a COSHH assessment. (See the Risk section)

- If you do get an external pest control company to come in, you need to know where the locations and quantities of any pesticides are. These should be mapped and documented in your pest management folder.

- If you are having repeated issues with certain pests, for example, you find an outbreak of cockroaches in the downstairs toilet every 3 months, your pest management folder can help you spot this. We would recommend delving into the source of this more deeply to eradicate the root cause.

FOOD HANDLING AND PEST CONTROL

Get help when you need it

Trained pest control teams are on hand to help, if you need to tackle a pest problem quickly and thoroughly. Or you can opt for one of our customised pest management programmes. One helps you set up and manage your own programme at your property. The other is where trained pest controllers comprehensively deals with all aspects of your pest management for you, giving you total peace of mind.

"Everyone deserves to live, work and thrive in a safe and secure environment."

Michael Coates

ACCOUNTABILITY

COMBAT
PEST CONTROL

ACCOUNTABILITY

Accountability is about deciding who is going to do what. And making changes to ensure the problem doesn't return.

Start by thinking about what you've learned in the System and Education chapter and answer these simple questions:

1   What am I doing now to create an environment that could harbour 1 or more pest species?

2   What can I change?

3   What do I need to resolve any problems or prevent an infestation?

4   Who can help me achieve this?

5   How long will it take?

6   When will it happen?

7   What do I need to do to maintain a safe, pest-free environment?

Let's address each question in turn.

1   What am I doing now to create an environment that could harbour 1 or more pest species?

This is very straightforward and requires nothing more than the Education chapter and some common sense.

Things to consider:

- Do you store waste/refuse in open containers (not a wheelie bin or bin with lid)?
- Do you leave waste bags containing food outside overnight?
- Do you have a compost heap?
- Is your garden overgrown?
- Do you leave food around your home (open packages, crumbs around the toaster, sweets in bedroom etc)?
- Is your housekeeping and hygiene a poor standard?
- Is there standing water in or around your home?
- Do you feed wildlife (birds, foxes, squirrels etc)?

If you've answered yes to any of the questions above, you will have identified one factor to change in order to discourage pests in and around your home.

One final tip – make sure you vacuum and clean your mattress and bedframe.

2 What can I change?

Depending on your answers above, you may need to change the way you store your waste. Or set a reminder to stay on top of garden maintenance. It could be that you need to implement an improved cleaning system – wiping food preparation surfaces after you've used them. Or stop feeding the wildlife in your area.

The key question to ask is: am I providing food, water and somewhere to live to a pest. If so, what am I doing? For step by step advice on how to control pests, flip to the Control chapter on p124.

3 What do I need to resolve any problems or prevent an infestation?

The answer to this will depend on the pest problem you have. But asking yourself this question will help you fix the issue fast and prevent it happening again.

The answer can range from things like:

- Purchase air vent covers to fit to external air bricks
- Contact the local authority about appropriate bins.
- Get professional help (see the 'Help' chapter).

4 Who can help me achieve this?

For the basics, start with your family:

- Is the issue waste-related? Make sure everyone knows that the bin bags need to be stored in the wheelie bin or secure waste area. If these aren't available, the bins should only be set out on the morning of bin collection.

- Need to start storing food more securely? Get everyone on board with how and where to store dry food like pasta, cereals, biscuits, bread etc. And ensure that everyone wipes down the food preparation surfaces every time they are used. No crumbs, fewer pests.

If you live in rented accommodation, you can seek advice from your housing trust or landlord – especially if you require professional assistance or if you feel structural work needs to be carried out.

5 How long will it take?

Estimate how long will it take you or someone else to complete the works.

6 When will it happen?

If you're carrying out the work yourself, you'll be in control of when this will happen. If you've arranged for a pest control company to help (or your landlord has arranged it), you'll need to be around to let them in and make sure the technicians can access everything they need to.

The pest control company should confirm the date, time and who will be attending in advance of the appointment.

7 What do I need to do to maintain a safe, pest-free environment?

Simple. To prevent a pest, make sure you remove their food source, water source and harbourage. In short, make your home as uninhabitable as possible for a pest.

RISK (AND HAZARDS)

COMBAT
PEST CONTROL

RISK (AND HAZARDS)

Okay, let's talk about risk.

Risks and hazards are two different things:
- **HAZARD is something that can cause you or others harm.**
- **RISK is the likelihood of the hazard causing you harm.**

We can alleviate the hazards by having good control measures (see Control chapter).

Hazards and their associated risks are classified in severity with the range (low to high):

Trivial – Minor injury – Over 3 day injury – Major injury/condition – Incapacity/death

Risks are also graded by probability:

Highly unlikely – Unlikely – Possible – Probable – Certain.

We aim to keep both probability and severity as close to 'Unlikely and Trivial' as possible.

Please note: This section (alongside the Control section) does not constitute a formal risk assessment and is to be used as a guideline only. Please seek professional assistance if needed and especially when your own competency is exhausted.

Here is a simple example of risks and hazards:
- Working near rodents can be a hazard.
- The risk of personal danger can be high.
- Rodent faeces is a hazard due to its ability to spread pathogens and disease.
- If the droppings are present whilst working and the pathogens/disease are ingested/inhaled etc then this becomes high risk.

For ways to reduce risk, please read the Control section.

Ok, so you now have an understanding of the basics. Let's look at each form of hazard that poses a risk.

There are 6 hazard categories:
- Physical
- Chemical
- Ergonomic
- Psychological
- Biological
- Radiation

We'll look at each one briefly, with a brief pest control example.

RISK (AND HAZARDS)

Physical – Slips, trips, falls, unsafe use of equipment, fire, exposure to chronic noise pollution, poor lighting.

As a professional pest control organisation, we aim to limit physical hazards through good working practices (and a bit of common sense). But the one to highlight when it comes to pests is fire. Now, this might not seem obvious, but rodents frequently gnaw through electrical wiring, presenting a very real fire risk.

Chemical – Dusts, gases, vapours, liquids, fumes.

At times, within our industry, it is appropriate to use pesticides. Rodenticides and insecticides can be hazardous, so please seek professional assistance but DIY products such as expanding foam will also contain hazardous substances. Do follow the instructions carefully.

Ergonomic – Poor design of equipment, repetitive movements, manual handling.

The main hazard when it comes to pest control is manual handling. That could mean moving a sofa or pulling a dishwasher out to inspect for rodents. Only lift or move what you are physically capable of lifting or moving. Attending a manual handling course is recommended and if in doubt, seek help.

Psychological – Dealing with noise/danger/ stress, made to feel unsafe or discriminated etc

A hazard that is hugely overlooked by most people is the psychological stress and trauma you go through while dealing with a pest infestation.

Having to live or work alongside Rats, Mice, Pigeons or Bedbugs can, and does, cause major psychological problems. This could be due to phobias or the emotional pain of sleeping in a bed that you know contains parasites such as Bedbugs.

We find the pests that cause most problems are Bedbugs, Rats, Mice, Pigeons, Fleas and Squirrels. That's because they are the most intrusive pests in your home. They can also cause interruptions to your sleep, which in turn, has a negative impact on your wellbeing and happiness.

We regularly come across clients who are experiencing heightened awareness, anxiety and in some cases, depression, because of an infestation.

Biological – Bacteria, pathogens, fungi, parasites through cuts especially to hands, insect/rodent bite, coming into contact with a contaminated object.

Another hazard high on our agenda. There is a plethora of pathogens and bacteria that can be transmitted due to the presence of pests. Please read the Control chapter for more specifics but for now take this advice: good hygiene is imperative to help control any contamination.

Radiation – Covers microwaves, lasers, x-rays, infra-red etc

Of all the hazards, this is the least likely one we'll come across in the fight against pests.

The Law – A final risk to be aware of is the law. Below, I've set out several acts and other guidelines and best practise points to be aware of.

LEGISLATION RELEVANT TO THE MANAGEMENT OF PESTS

- **Prevention of Damage by Pest Act 1949**

  Definition of negligence; Implications if pest controller or company found to be negligent.

  What it means for you: This gives local authorities the power to deal with a pest issue on behalf of a 3rd party, cost would be recovered.

- **Food and Environment Protection Act 1985**

  Part 3: Control of Pesticides Regulations 1986 and Biocidal Product Regulation (BPR, Regulation (EU) 528/2012).

  What it means for you: Only use products approved by the above.

- **Public Health Act 1961**

  Disconnection and sealing of disused drains.

  Specified urban birds (Mainly Pigeons and their guano).

  What it means for you: Gives the local authorities the power to deal with feral Pigeons in built up areas.

- **The Housing Act 2004**

  What it means for you: Residential Premises should provide a safe and healthy environment for any potential occupant or visitor.

- **Pest Act 1954**

  What it means for you: Only certain types of spring traps are approved for killing/taking animals. These are listed in, Spring Traps Approval (England) Order 2012.

  Spread of Myxomatosis. It is illegal to use an infected rabbit to spread this disease.

- **Public Health Act 1936**

  What it means for you: This Act concerns the destruction or removal of vermin – mostly in regards to the removal and destruction of bedbugs. This Act gave the local councils the authority to enter homes and deal with the infestation, as well as remove wallpaper and furniture that is affected.

LEGISLATION RELEVANT TO THE MANAGEMENT OF PESTS

- **Protection of Animals Act 1911–1927**

  What it means for you: This Act concerns the prevention of cruelty to animals. Do not cause unnecessary suffering, beat, torture, burn, suffocate an animal or perform any operation without due care and humanity.

- **Animals Cruel Poisons Act 1962**

  What it means for you: The use of any poison for the purpose of destroying any animal has been prohibited or restricted.

- **Environmental Protection Act 1990**

  What it means for you: This Act prevents:
  - The use of Audible bird scarers near residential areas
  - Disposal of pesticides and other waste
  - Prosecutions can occur where the presence of pest can be classified as being a danger to health.

- **Clean Neighbourhood & Environment Act 2005**

  What it means for you: This Act concerns any insects emanating from industrial, trade or business premises being prejudicial to health or a nuisance.

- **Wildlife and Countryside Act 1981**

  What it means for you:
  - Protection of flora and fauna.
  - Protects all birds.
  - Protects all bats.
  - Permitted methods of control. Lists illegal methods of killing: Bows, Crossbows, and Explosives etc.

- **Food Safety Act 1990**

  What it means for you: Officers can close premises under 'Due Diligence' and prevent the sale of unfit food.

- **Food Hygiene Regulations 2013**

  What it means for you:

  - By law, you must prevent pest infestations and control pests in food premises and near equipment.
  - Food safety legislation states, owners of food premises must periodically visually check for signs of pests and have a pest control reporting system in place.

- **Health and Safety at Work Act 1974**

  Who's responsible:

  - Employers
  - Self Employed
  - Employees
  - Any person

- **Control of Substances Hazardous to Health Regulations 2002**

  What it means for you:

  - COSHH assessments should be carried out whenever dealing with hazardous substances.
  - Companies with less than 5 employees are not required to keep written records.

LEGISLATION RELEVANT TO THE MANAGEMENT OF PESTS

- **Campaign Responsible Rodenticide Use (CRRU) UK Code of Best Practice**

  Rodent control guidance for professionals.

  Sensible use of SGARs as not to poison non target species.

  CRRU was based on the below HSE sheets.

  Health safety executive (HSE) (1999). Safe use of rodenticides on farms and holdings

  HSE (2004). Urban rodent control and safe use of rodenticides by professional users.

  Rodenticides should always be the last resort.

  Risk Hierarchy. The steps taken when dealing with an infestation.

- **Environmental Risk Assessment**

  This should be carried out whenever a risk to the environment has been identified during the site survey.

  Points to assess and document:

  a   What the treatment is designed to achieve, methods of rodent control

  b   Protected species that may be present or near

  c   Any risks to non-target species

  d   Facilities for disposal of dead bodies

  e   Persons responsible for infested site

  f   Follow up measures

  g   Any environmental management measures to make site less attractive to rodents once infestation has been dealt with.

It is good practice to record this assessment in writing.

CONTROL

CONTROL

Now you understand the risks and hazards involved in dealing with your pest infestation, it's time to control them.

This chapter has two parts. The first helps you understand the theory of controlling pests.

The second part gives you step-by-step instructions on how to control the most common domestic pests.

PART 1: THE THEORY

When it comes to tackling a pest infestation, we use the Hierarchy of Control. It helps to eliminate the exposure any person or team has to hazards. Put simply, it allows you to control the situation in the safest way possible.

The Hierarchy of Control is a tried and tested strategy in most industries. I certainly followed it in the military and fire service.

It has a set order and must be followed in this sequence for maximum benefit.

1 Elimination
2 Substitution
3 Engineering controls
4 Administrative controls
5 Personal protective equipment

Each control measure takes you closer to the hazard. To explain each step, I've used the example of controlling a rat infestation. But you can skip to part 2 for the full lowdown on how to control other common pests.

1 Elimination

This means physically removing the hazard if possible.

Pest control example: The bird feeder is providing a food source for the rats. To eliminate the hazard, remove the bird feeder.

2 Substitution

The next step is to replace the hazard with something that doesn't pose the same or any risk.

Pest Control example: If you're using a table-top style bird feeder, which stands in the garden, the danger is that rats run up the leg of the feeder and on to the table top.

Substitute your table-top bird feeder with hanging feeder.

Another professional way is to substitute the rat's food with rodenticide. This will help control an infestation but must be carried out by a professional pest control organisation and will involve safeguards around protecting non-target species like birds.

3 Engineering Control

This step does not eliminate the hazard but helps to protect you from it.

Pest control example: My home is in a busy town centre, located near public bins. Rats have been seen feeding from the bins and have entered my property under the front door, which has a 2cm gap at the bottom.

CONTROL

When you engineer control, you can take steps to proof your door and prevent the rat from entering. You'll need to choose a material that cannot be gnawed through (steel plate for example). This will help protect you (and your home) from the hazard. Though the rats will still frequent the bins unless further action is taken.

4 Administrative Control

This is all about changing the way people behave.

Pest control example: We are in a large block with 50 separate flats. A communal waste area is attached to the block and has seen a sudden and severe infestation of rats.

Residents have been leaving their bin bags on the floor of the waste area instead of placing them securely in the industrial bins provided.

Using administrative control means educating residents to change their behaviour. If you manage the building, provide posters and send a letter to each resident explaining that this behaviour needs to change to help maintain a pest-free environment.

5 Personal protective equipment

This is the last resort. At this stage, you are tackling the hazard head-on. You'll need gloves, coveralls, safety boots, hard hats etc. It is the least preferred control measure as the likelihood of hazard exposure is high. If it gets to this stage, we recommend seeking assistance from a professional pest control company.

Pest control example: Rat droppings found in kitchen. Gloves, coveralls and full-face respirator need to be used to clean up droppings and disinfect using medical grade cleaning agent. This is because rat faeces can contain pathogens and spreads diseases. The level of risk to humans is high.

PART 2: HOW TO CONTROL (OR GET RID OF) COMMON PESTS

In this section you'll find simple step-by-step instructions on how to deal with an infestation.

In almost every instance, the key is to identify and remove the food source, water source and shelter.

Rat

1 Survey the site, record what you see. Take pictures of your findings, write a diary of rodent activity and draw a map of possible problem locations.

2 Next, remove all possible food sources. Place food stuffs like pasta, bread and fresh food in sealed plastic containers and place them out of reach. If it's outside, place bird seed and pet food in sealed plastic containers.

3 Clear and clean areas you feel could be providing harbourage (the rats nest or potential nest area).

4 Are there areas outside or near your property that could be harbouring pests? For example, is your garden overgrown? Or is there waste accumulating in an area near your home? Rats will make a home in empty boxes or feast on leftover rubbish.

5 Remove water sources. Is there a leaking pipe? Or some standing water inside or outside? Fix or remove it.

6 Proofing the area is always advised but ensure you seal everything in a thorough and effective manner – systemise your treatment. Failure to do this could result in a more complicated job if you ever call for professional help.

Mice

1 Survey the site, record what you see. Take pictures of your findings, write a diary of rodent activity and draw a map of possible problem locations.

2 Next, remove all possible food sources. Place food stuffs like pasta, bread and fresh food in sealed plastic containers and place them out of reach. If it's outside, place bird seed and pet food in sealed plastic containers.

3 Clear and clean areas you feel could be providing harbourage (the mouse nest or potential nest area).

4 Ensure you vacuum the areas in which you have prepared or eaten food, even a tiny amount can be enough to attract and sustain a mouse.

5 Have a deep clean, especially in boiler cupboards and storage under the stairs. Mice love warm places. A good tidy will ensure that no nests have been made.

6 Proofing the area is always advised but ensure you seal everything in a thorough and effective manner – systemise your treatment. Failure to do this could result in a more complicated job if you ever call for professional help.

7 Baiting using rodenticide is a great way of controlling mice, however, I would recommend this is done by a reputable and accredited pest control professional.

CONTROL

Clothes Moth

1 Prevent clothes moths by vacuuming regularly. If you have an infestation, this can greatly reduce moth/larvae numbers. Remember to vacuum areas that are often missed like under beds and behind cupboards.

2 If you have animal based clothing (wool, leather, furs) use pheromone traps to monitor the areas you store the garments.

3 Regular inspection of stored clothing (the winter/summer wardrobe) can be a great way to locate and quickly prevent an infestation spreading.

4 Freeze affected items of clothing for approximately 2 days. And monitor thereafter.

5 Although it's expensive, dry cleaning can help prevent moth larvae devouring items of clothing. Well worth it to save your favourite cashmere jumper.

6 Infestations can and do occur because people bring new/infested items of clothing into their properties. So if you've received a jumper, cardigan, skirt, coat etc which might be attractive to moths (wool, leather, fur), check it for evidence of moths and quarantine it if you find anything.

7 Check the loft. We regularly find severe infestations have one or two main high quality food sources. Generally it is a fabric that is out of sight. Often we find old wool based carpet (stored in the attic) full of all the stages of the moth life cycle.

Bedbugs

1 The best way to deal with bedbugs is to prevent them getting into your property in the first place. Check hotel rooms, hostel beds for signs if you are away from home (see below).

2 Wash your clothes when you get back from travelling (+60 degrees).

3 Inspect travel bags, rucksacks etc. Pay close attention to the seams.

4 Good housekeeping in your property: regularly clean, vacuum mattresses, under bed, bed frame, sofas, chairs etc. If you notice anything please follow stages below.

5 Vacuum all areas. Especially areas of concern like the mattress, sofa, bed frame, carpet, cracks and crevices.

6 Wash all bedding and other items that have been exposed at +60 degrees (freeze or dry cleaning are other viable options). Ensure you bag up the items ready for wash and do not put cleaned, dry items back until infested areas have been treated.

7 Research appropriate DIY treatments if this is the path which you wish to take. They range widely and can include, steam, heat or chemical methods.

8 Treat the whole property 2-3 times over a period of around 3-4 weeks. It's essential you use a residual insecticide or dust the area using a broad spectrum of treatments available. Please ensure you follow product guidelines with respect to usage and personal protective equipment. I can't stress enough how important it is to protect yourself at this stage. Seek professional help if you need to.

9 Keep monitoring after treatment with regular inspections of the problem area.

Fleas

1 **Vacuum thoroughly** – especially around areas where your pet would sleep/spend time (immediately empty bag/container once you're finished).

2 **Bag up** – all affected fabrics. Place into waste bags, tie a knot (cable tie) until they are ready to be washed.

3 **Wash** – wash all bedding and fabrics that have been affected. Use the washing machine setting of at least 60 degrees. Once dry, put away in a treated area or back into a new waste bag until the area is treated and free of fleas.

4 **Use a wet flea treatment** (insecticide or equivalent) – residual treatments work best but you must always read the guidelines, especially regarding safety requirement. This might include protective equipment (respiratory protection, gloves etc). If in doubt, contact a pest control expert (NPTA is a great place to find an accredited individual/company).

5 **Powder** – is another good way of ensuring longterm protection. Usually place around the edges of rooms. As per step 4, it's crucial that you follow the guidelines, especially around using protective equipment.

6 **Spot on** – this is a medicated pet treatment designed specifically for your dog, cat, rabbit etc. Before using it, seek professional assistance from your vet. Follow the advice and keep on top of this. This will help to prevent re-infestations (especially during summer months).

7 **Monitor** – place monitoring traps around the property, especially around areas of concern.

CONTROL

Cockroaches (Oriental) and (German)

Oriental Cockroaches

1   Remove all available food sources. Check under kitchen appliances, remove grease around ovens and put edible food stuffs in sealed containers.

2   Use a bait (edible that reacts in the stomach). This is by far the best way of controlling a population, especially if applied in/around their harbourage.

3   Repair any broken tiles, flooring, worktops etc (seal with silicon, mastic or equivalent).

4   Clean, clean and clean all areas of concern.

5   Repeat steps 1, 2 and 3. Oriental cockroaches can take time and repeated treatments are almost always appropriate.

German Cockroaches

1   Remove all available food sources. Check under kitchen appliances, remove grease around ovens and but edible food stuffs in sealed containers. Venture higher up with the German as they are great climbers. So look at food on top of cupboards/fridges etc.

2   Use a bait (edible that reacts in the stomach). This is by far the best way of controlling a population, especially if applied in/around their harbourage.

3   Wet spray insecticide can be used in adjoining rooms.

4   Clean/inspect areas throughout treatment. Monitoring traps can be used but visual checks will show what's actually going on.

Squirrel

1 If you have put out food in your garden for them, or even for the birds, it's time to stop feeding them. By luring the grey squirrel into your garden, you could vastly increase the chances of them using your home as a hotel.

2 Trim any tree/hedge etc that is touching your property. If a tree's branches are draped over your roof, you're giving the squirrel an easy access point to enter your home. Make the area hostile and uninviting. (Please take note: some trees have conservation orders on them so please speak to the relevant organisations – tree council.org.uk is a good start).

3 Proof all entry points – especially around the fascia and gutters. Squirrels will also gain entry through inviting gaps around bathroom extractor fan outlets and broken roof tiles. Good maintenance and repair is vital (please note: for your safety, you must always use correct and safe working platforms when working at height. Also use competent persons and if in doubt, speak to a professional).

Wasp

Please consider these 5 points before dealing with a nest.

1 **Allergies** – is anyone in the building allergic to wasp stings? If so, please seek professional assistance.

2 **Equipment** – you will need a full bee keepers suit including gloves. If you're working at height, a safe working platform and training may be needed. Better still, invest in a telescopic lance and take away the risk of a fall.

3 **Treatment** – make sure you use an appropriate insecticide that treats the full nest, not just a few individuals. Read the instructions. Please remember, once treatment has happened the wasps within the nest are very likely to become extremely aggressive.

4 **Emergency** – have a plan in case you or anyone around you gets stung. Seek medical attention immediately, understand and know what you have to do before it happens (assess the risk).

5 **Keep away** – from the area of the nest for a period of time. 4 hours to several days depending on what time of the year/how big the nest/how effective the treatment has been. Close all windows and doors around the treated area. Inform neighbours about your intentions regarding treatment.

CONTROL

Ants

1   With ants, it's all about prevention. Ensure all sweet food is placed in a sealed container, preferably airtight.

2   Have a spring clean – especially in kitchen cupboards.

3   Clean all food preparation areas on a daily basis (minimum), especially during the summer months.

4   Garden ants are an indicator that the external part of your home is in good shape i.e you have a healthy garden. But if ants do gain entry the first thing you should do is attempt to seal their entry points. Generally using mortar, cement, silicon etc will be enough to secure your home.

5   If the invasion persists, then the dual use of a powder and bait insecticide is advised. Your main priority is to control the nest not just a few individuals. Many DIY treatments only deal with short term solutions. If in doubt, contact a professional pest control company.

6   All treatment can take several weeks to take effect depending on the size of nest, effectiveness of application, weather conditions etc. So please be patient.

Cluster flies

It's hard to prevent cluster flies as these tricky customers can and will gain entry into loft spaces through the smallest of entry points. To seal an area like a loft can be unreasonable especially as these areas often need ventilation and air flow.

You can use traps and electric fly killers. But the best thing to do is seek professional assistance.

Blow flies

Prevention

1 Keep meat waste in a sealed container, better still keep it in a sealed container that is kept refrigerated until the day of the waste collection.

2 If your pet uses an area of your garden/patio as a toilet, pick up and dispose of faeces, minimum of once per day.

3 Cover all meat food sources when left out of the fridge.

Additional Prevention for food handling premises

1 Fit fly screens/mesh on windows and external doors.

2 Consider the location of an electric fly killer (ELK). Not in line of sight of windows, door etc – we don't want to attract flies in.

Treatment

1 Remove any rodent/bird carcasses (typical if you have a rodent infestation that has used bait and if you have pigeons living within the property).

2 Ensure all maggots have been collected and disposed of.

3 Use an appropriate aerosol insecticide and/or a wet spray residual if large numbers of flies are settling in one area. Always read, understand and implement the relevant safety precautions on each product.

4 If in doubt, speak to a professional pest controller.

Fruit flies

1 Remove overripe fruit and vegetables.

2 Remove fermented materials like beer and soft drinks.

3 Clean areas where fruit, vegetables, beer and soft drink residues are present – even a small spill on a kitchen bench or food preparation area is enough to attract them.

4 Empty food waste recycling bins and keep them clean.

CONTROL

Drain Flies

1 **Prevent** – Clean/clear your drains, plugs holes, system traps etc, anywhere that sludge can build up.

2 **Knockdown** – sprays bought in a DIY shop can help control any immediate 'flying infestation (read the product instructions before use).

3 **Locate** – the source of the infestation (plug holes, internal manhole covers for sewage etc).

4 **Remove** – the breeding area. Clean/clear the traps, pipes etc. Use water, eco cleaning products, scrubbing brushes. The area should have a deep clean.

5 **Maintenance** – if the issue persists, you may need to replace your pipes or even the sinks. Clean areas at least monthly with a drain cleaning agent of your choice.

Foxes

1 Ensure areas around outbuildings are free from foliage and rubble. Keep these areas clear.

2 Keep your waste secure. Metal bins are a great way to keep foxes away from your unwanted food.

3 Proof around the base of your shed. Leave no gaps, especially if the structure has been built on top of earth.

4 Use a repellent to deter foxes further. These can be bought online and require thorough treatments on a regular basis. Your job is to recreate a territory – and to become the dominant fox.

5 And the last tip: don't feed foxes! They will look after themselves.

Feral Pigeon

1   Remove all food. Now this might be (song) bird feed in the garden, waste bins that have been ripped apart by foxes leaving food waste or neighbours feeding them intentionally. The first thing to do is to stop their food.

2   Second, exclude or deter the birds. If your house is now their house, you will have to put a control measure in place to prevent their access.

3   Last thing is to clean up all guano (pigeon poo) – this is a hazard which can spread disease. Use a bio-hazard spill kit, water pressure alongside a disinfectant.

4   Please seek professional assistance if an infestation has occurred.

HELP

If you need help to tackle a pest infestation, please feel free to get in touch. You can call us on 0208 6225 317.

We hope this book has helped you, whether you want to become a stronger leader, create an interdependent culture that helps your team thrive or live a happier, pest-free life.

We believe passionately about helping others and also positively contributing to the communities we live and work in.

Find us online:

 @hqcombat or
@michael__coates

 Visit us: warandpest.com
and combatpestcontrol.com

 Watch us: youtube.com
(Search for Combat Pest Control)

 Listen to us: declassifiedpodcast.com

For further information on managing pests:

- National Pest Technicians Association (NPTA)
- Natural England
- British Pest Control Association (BPCA)
- Royal Society for Public Health (RSPH)
- Chartered Institute of Environmental Health (CIEH)

OBSERVATIONS

_____
_____
_____
_____

INFESTATION RATING

(0) (1) (2) (3) (4) (5) (6) (7) (8) (9) (10)

ACTIONS

_____
_____
_____
_____

TREATMENT

_____
_____
_____
_____

MONTHLY MANAGEMENT

_____
_____
_____
_____

RECOMMENDATIONS

_____
_____
_____
_____

TECHNICIAN NOTES FOR NEXT VISIT

_____
_____
_____
_____

A Combat Pest Control technician has attended. The client is happy that thorough and responsible
pest managment has taken place. [ ]
The site was left in good order / repair, pictures taken, a report was left and client has been briefed. [ ]

Customer Name: _____
Customer Signature: _____
Date: _____

Technician Name: _____
Technician Signature: _____
Date: _____

COMBAT - TREATMENT REPORT - **CPC** _____ NAME _____ DATE / /

OBSERVATIONS

_____
_____
_____
_____
_____

INFESTATION RATING

(0) (1) (2) (3) (4) (5) (6) (7) (8) (9) (10)

ACTIONS

_____
_____
_____
_____
_____

TREATMENT

_____
_____
_____
_____

MONTHLY MANAGEMENT

_____
_____
_____
_____
_____

RECOMMENDATIONS

_____
_____
_____
_____

TECHNICIAN NOTES FOR NEXT VISIT

_____
_____
_____
_____

A Combat Pest Control technician has attended. The client is happy that thorough and responsible pest managment has taken place. [ ]
The site was left in good order / repair, pictures taken, a report was left and client has been briefed. [ ]

Customer Name: _____ Technician Name: _____

Customer Signature: _____ Technician Signature: _____

Date: _____ Date: _____

EMPLOY   EDUCATE   PROTECT   SUPPORT

COMBAT - TREATMENT REPORT - **CPC** _____ NAME _____ DATE / /

OBSERVATIONS

_____
_____
_____
_____
_____

INFESTATION RATING   (0) (1) (2) (3) (4) (5) (6) (7) (8) (9) (10)

ACTIONS

_____
_____
_____
_____
_____

TREATMENT

_____ _____ _____ _____ _____ _____
_____ _____ _____ _____ _____ _____
_____ _____ _____ _____ _____ _____
_____ _____ _____ _____ _____ _____

MONTHLY MANAGEMENT

_____
_____
_____
_____
_____

RECOMMENDATIONS   TECHNICIAN NOTES FOR NEXT VISIT

_____   _____
_____   _____
_____   _____
_____   _____

[✓] A Combat Pest Control technician has attended. The client is happy that thorough and responsible
pest managment has taken place. { }
The site was left in good order / repair, pictures taken, a report was left and client has been briefed. { }

Customer Name: _____   Technician Name: _____
Customer Signature: _____   Technician Signature: _____
Date: _____   Date: _____

EMPLOY   EDUCATE   PROTECT   SUPPORT

COMBAT - TREATMENT REPORT - **CPC**   NAME _____   DATE / /

OBSERVATIONS

_____
_____
_____
_____

INFESTATION RATING   (0) (1) (2) (3) (4) (5) (6) (7) (8) (9) (10)

ACTIONS

_____
_____
_____
_____

TREATMENT

____ ____ ____ ____ ____ ____
____ ____ ____ ____ ____ ____
____ ____ ____ ____ ____ ____
____ ____ ____ ____ ____ ____

MONTHLY MANAGEMENT

_____
_____
_____
_____

RECOMMENDATIONS   ### TECHNICIAN NOTES FOR NEXT VISIT

_____   _____
_____   _____
_____   _____
_____   _____

☑ A Combat Pest Control technician has attended. The client is happy that thorough and responsible
pest managment has taken place. [ ]
The site was left in good order / repair, pictures taken, a report was left and client has been briefed. [ ]

Customer Name: _____   Technician Name: _____

Customer Signature: _____   Technician Signature: _____

Date: _____   Date: _____

COMBAT - TREATMENT REPORT - **CPC** _____ NAME _____ DATE / /

COMBAT – THE MAP

PLAN

COMBAT - TREATMENT REPORT - **CPC**   NAME _____   DATE / /

OBSERVATIONS

_____
_____
_____
_____
_____

INFESTATION RATING   (0) (1) (2) (3) (4) (5) (6) (7) (8) (9) (10)

ACTIONS

_____
_____
_____
_____
_____

TREATMENT

_____
_____
_____
_____

MONTHLY MANAGEMENT

_____
_____
_____
_____
_____

RECOMMENDATIONS   TECHNICIAN NOTES FOR NEXT VISIT

_____   _____
_____   _____
_____   _____
_____   _____

[✓] A Combat Pest Control technician has attended. The client is happy that thorough and responsible pest managment has taken place. [ ]
The site was left in good order / repair, pictures taken, a report was left and client has been briefed. [ ]

Customer Name: _____   Technician Name: _____

Customer Signature: _____   Technician Signature: _____

Date: _____   Date: _____

EMPLOY   EDUCATE   PROTECT   SUPPORT

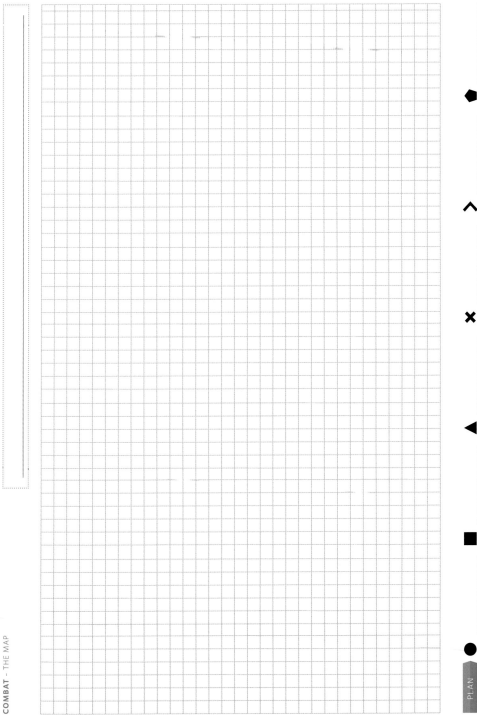

COMBAT - TREATMENT REPORT - **CPC** _____ NAME _____ DATE / /

OBSERVATIONS

_____
_____
_____
_____
_____

INFESTATION RATING   (0) (1) (2) (3) (4) (5) (6) (7) (8) (9) (10)

ACTIONS

_____
_____
_____
_____

TREATMENT

____ _____ _____ _____ _____ ____
____ _____ _____ _____ _____ ____
____ _____ _____ _____ _____ ____
____ _____ _____ _____ _____ ____

MONTHLY MANAGEMENT

_____
_____
_____
_____

RECOMMENDATIONS   ## TECHNICIAN NOTES FOR NEXT VISIT

_____   _____
_____   _____
_____   _____
_____   _____

✓ A Combat Pest Control technician has attended. The client is happy that thorough and responsible
   pest managment has taken place. [ ]
   The site was left in good order / repair, pictures taken, a report was left and client has been briefed. [ ]

Customer Name: _____   Technician Name: _____

Customer Signature: _____   Technician Signature: _____

Date: _____   Date: _____

EMPLOY   EDUCATE   PROTECT   SUPPORT

COMBAT
PEST CONTROL

ACKNOWLEDGEMENTS

WAR AND **PEST**

ACKNOWLEDGEMENTS

I would like to thank the hundreds of members of the Armed Forces and emergency services I have worked with. Your constant input over the years has been amazing especially 35 Engineer Regiment and White Watch. Since starting in business we've had endless help and support. To name a few – my brother Gary, my Mam, Captain of industry Dan G, Sarah S, Emma C, Olly, Gresty, Shirley, Matt, Paul & Masami, Glen and Daniel, Jeanne, Mark M, Graeme S, Mark S, Ant C, Jacqui T, Stephen C, Ted, Rick, Doug, Paul, Tony, Jase S, Pat P, Gaz R, Anna L, Gary B, and all at the DRM, Trudy, all our great clients, members of the veteran and business community who have helped and guide me also.

Thanks to Beth, all the guests of the podcast and Steve B and HESCO and all who have listened and contributed.

Helene has and continues to be next to me every step of the way as does A, P and M.

I'd like to thank all the past, current and future Combat Team including Mike B, Chris, Dan, Carl, Lee and Amie.

Biggest thank you is to Des. We joined the British Army on the same day, same trade, posted to Germany and deployed twice to Iraq together, played rugby, ran, walked, then went into business to make an impact. A good start and great things to come.

One last thing, not usually sentimental but I would like to dedicate this book to my Dad, I know he would have been proud.

What's next?

To find out how we can help managers and providers with social housing, simply complete the digital score card at scorecard. **www.combatpestcontrol.com**

To arrange a 'Protect your residents' meeting with Michael, simply email: **bookings@combatpestcontrol.com**

If you've enjoyed your read, spread the word. Leave a review of the book on Amazon.

For more life-changing military stories, listen to an episode of the podcast at: **www.declassifiedpodcast.com**

Live by your values, lead by example and enjoy life.

THE AUTHOR

THE AUTHOR

Michael joined the British Army aged 16, serving nearly six years with the Royal Engineers. During his service, he spent time in Iraq at the beginning of 2003 and then again at the end of the year. Once he returned to civilian life, Michael spent 9 years in the Fire Service.

After witnessing several of his friends and peers suffer from post-traumatic stress disorder, following their time in conflict, Michael felt compelled to help his fellow Military Veterans.

Michael started Combat Pest Control in 2015 with his friend and fellow veteran Des. Since then they are one of only a handful of organisations to have won the Ministry of Defence Gold award in employer recognition, at the time the youngest and smallest company to have won this award.

Combat Pest Control has provided over 40,000 days of clean drinking water and several thousand days of education to children in conflict and continue to clear minefields through their partnership with APOPO.

Michael is also the host of the life-changing podcast 'Declassified' which documents military stories to provide help, support and guidance to individuals suffering from both physical illness and injury.

He is also the international bestselling co-author of – 'Better Business, Better Life, Better World – The Movement'.

Michael is also a regular corporate speaker, who has flown round the world sharing stories and lessons around leadership, values, interdependency and how small business can make a huge impact.

Clients have included:

- Ministry of Defence
- FDM group
- Deloitte LLP
- Buy1 Give1
- Hull City Council
- Surrey Council Social Services
- Fair tax
- Combat Stress

Michael is a keen endurance athlete, former rugby player who lives with his family in West London.

NOTES

NOTES

NOTES

NOTES

What does it take to become a better leader?
And how do you build a culture where every
team member is empowered to be their best?
Can a business not only survive – but thrive –
by prioritising values over value?

This book arms you with all you need to know
to transform your team and achieve your goals.

Follow the SEARCH methodology to become a
better leader, create an interdependent culture
and change the world for the better.

Plus, it shows how the SEARCH methodology
works in the pest industry. Giving you easy to
follow steps to tackle troublesome invasions.
And valuable insights into the secret lives of
pests – from a team of those who have served
in the British Military.